ALLELOPATHIC POTENTIAL OF SOME SPECIES OF FAMILY CUCURBITACEAE

ALLELOCHEMICALS IDENTIFIED IN SELECTED PLANTS OF FAMILY CUCURBITACEAE.

DR. YOGESH RAGHUNATH AHIRE

Copyright © Dr. Yogesh Raghunath Ahire
All Rights Reserved.

This Book is Dedicated

to

My Beloved Parents

Late Mr. Raghunath Shivram Ahire

Late Mrs. Jijabai Raghunath Ahire

Contents

Preface

In this book attempts have been made to investigate the allelopathic potency from the selected four species of family cucurbitaceae was examined on seed germination and seedling growth of *Phaseolus aconitifolius* Jacq. var – 'Abhaya'. During the survey it was observed that the selected weeds are noxious weeds in agricultural fields, which significantly reduce the crop yields. It was also observed that though these are the weeds the local people utilities them in various ailments of man and animals. The allelopathic potentials were tested and confirmed by using various techniques such as phytoextracts bioassay, leachates bioassay, root zone soil bioassay, decomposition bioassay and volatilization bioassay on selected plants.

In addition, soil analysis and detailed phytochemical screening were also carried out and supported to the results which have been obtained in different bioassays. After detailed studies it has been confirmed that these plants are having allelopathic potency as these have been expressed in the fields where they are found to be growing.

Acknowledgements

I express my deep sense of gratitude to my research guide Dr. S. S. Deokule, Professor, Department of Botany, University of Pune. I shall ever remain grateful for his inspiring and instructive guidance, valuable criticism and encouragement throughout the period of my work.

It would have been impossible for me to undertake and complete this work with the best wishes and giving me advice by my beloved wife Mrs. Gayatri Yogesh Ahire, my son Daksh and daughter Vedika.

.

Dr. Ahire Yogesh Raghunath

CHAPTER ONE

Introduction

We always felt that we need our own space. Sometimes we all need to be alone. All kinds of plants need to have their own space too. How do we get our own space? We can walk away or shut our door. But what can plants do? They can't walk or run anywhere. All living things need certain resources to live and grow. What does our body need to be healthy? Plants need sunlight, nutrients, water, and air. The roots bring nutrients and water from the ground for rest of the parts of plant. The leaves absorb the sun's rays for energy. When plants don't have enough space, they cannot meet their needs. So, the plants protect their resources by using process of allelopathy.

Allelopathy is a chemical process that a plant uses to keep other plants from growing too close or away from it. The word allelopathy derived from two separate words. The *allelon* which means "of each other", and *pathos* which means "to suffer". Allelopathy refers to the chemical inhibition of one species by another. The "inhibitory" chemicals releases into the environment where it affects the development and growth of neighboring plants. Allelopathic chemicals can be present in any part of the plant. They can be found in roots, stems, leaves, flowers or fruits. They can also be found in the surrounding soil. These toxins affect target species in many different ways. The toxic chemicals may inhibit root/shoot growth, they may inhibit nutrient uptake, or they may attack a naturally occurring symbiotic relationship thereby destroying the plant's usable source of a nutrient. Not all plants have allelopathic tendencies. Some, though they exhibit these tendencies, may actually be displaying aggressive competition of a non-chemical form. There may be much of the controversy surrounding to identifying allelopathy in trying to distinguish the type of competition being displayed. In general, if it is of a chemical nature, then the plant is considered allelopathic. There have been some recent links to plant allelotoxins directed at animals, but data is scarce.

Molisch in 1937 first coined the term allelopathy, which refer to biochemical interactions between all types of plants including microorganisms. The term allelopathy was derived from Greek word, which means mutual harm. This term covers both the detrimental and beneficial reciprocal biochemical interactions. Rice in 1984 also defined allelopathy as any direct or indirect, harmful or beneficial effect of one plant on another plant through release of chemicals into the environment. Allelopathy is the inhibition of growth of a plant due to biomolecules released by another. It is the opposite of symbiotic mutualism. The biomolecules are called *allelochemicals* and are produced by some plants as secondary metabolites. When the allelochemicals are released into the environment, they inhibit the development of neighboring plants. Allelochemicals were suspected in 19th century in agriculture because of many observations of 'soil sicknesses of farmlands. If a piece of farmland is continually cropped to one plant, the yields often decrease and cannot be improved by additional fertilizers. Fruit trees, for example, often do poorly in farm land where the same species has grown before. Furthermore, it is common for one plant to harm another plant grown in its vicinity a phenomenon called allelopathy. Allelochemicals refer mostly to be the secondary metabolites produced by plants and are by-products of primary metabolic growth and development of the same plant or neighboring plants. Some of them are accumulated at various stages of growth, while some depends upon time of day or season. There are hundreds of secondary metabolites in the plant kingdom and many are known to be *phytotoxic* (Einhellig, 2002). Allelopathic effects of these compounds are often observed to occur early in the life cycle, causing inhibition of seed germination and/or seedling growth. The compounds exhibit a wide range of mechanisms of action, from effects on DNA (alkaloids), photosynthetic and mitochondrial function (quinones), phytohormone activity, ion uptake, and water balance (*phenolics*). Interpretations of mechanisms of action are complicated by the fact that individual compounds can have multiple phytotoxic effects (Einhellig, 2002).

Allelochemicals selectively inhibit the growth of soil microorganisms or other plants or both. They play an important role in chemical warfare between plants (allelopathic interactions) and include natural herbicides, phytoallexins (microbial inhibitors) and inhibitors of seed germination. Although, many allelochemicals are strictly defensive substances, other is offensive compounds that act directly in weed aggressiveness, competition and the regulation of plant diversity (c.f. Avchar, 2005). It is expected that in the near future many allelochemicals may be used commercially as herbicides, insecticides and nematocides or as bio regulators. Allelochemicals most often impart plant resistance to insects, nematodes and pathogens; besides following their release into an environment, it may regulate the distribution and vigour of plants. Most often plants come in contact with the allelochemicals in soil and their effect on crop plants may be modified by soil moisture, soil temperature and other soil factors (Patrick & Koch, 1958; Patrick *et al.*, 1964; Wang *et al.*, 1967; McCalla and Norstadt, 1974; Bhowmik and Doll, 1983a & b; Einhellig & Eckrich, 1984). Some of the allelochemicals such as terpenoids and polyacetylenes may function in a volatile state, but most of the current research in agro systems involves water-soluble compounds. The known list of chemicals involved in allelopathy continues to expand and with better isolation and identification techniques, many new substances are being added. Grummer (1955) suggested that special terms be used for the chemical agents involved in allelopathy based on the type of plant producing the agent and the type of plant affected. He suggested the term antibiotic for a chemical agent produced by a micro-organisms, phytoncide for a chemicals produced by a higher plant and effective against a micro-organisms; marasmin for agents produced by micro-organisms and effective against higher plants; and kolin for a chemical agent produced by a higher plant and effective against higher plants. Organisms interact in many interesting ways. Chemicals produced by one organism that affect other organism are called allelochemicals (Krebs, 1978; Ricklefs, 1979 and Whittaker, 1975). Sometimes a single chemical produced by one organism is harmful to another organism but beneficial to third organism.

Allelopathy involves a complex chain of chemical communication between plant species (Harborne, 1987). Allelopathic interactions may also play a key role in influencing the distribution of vegetation in nature, the yield of various crop species and weed interference (Muller, 1966; Putnam and Duke, 1978; Kaminsky, 1981; Aldrich, 1984 and Rice, 1984). The significance of allelopathy to the ecological theory was highlighted by Muller (1966 and 1969). Even low qualities of a chemical may significantly influences plant growth, nutrient ion absorption and consequently micro-climate (Muller, 1966). Allelopathic interference include inhibitory and promoting effects (Rice, 1986). Usually secondary metabolites are involved in allelopathy. These chemicals are called allelochemicals. The term 'allelochemicals' derived from 'allelochemics', coined by Whittaker and Feeny (1971), and was first used by Chou and Waller in 1983. Since then, the term has been used in literature dealing with interspecific chemical interactions between organisms. In order to designate an allelochemicals, its release into or its origin in the environment must be demonstrated. Allelochemicals are released into the environment through leaching of living plant parts, root exudates, volatilization, residue decomposition, microbial activity, and agricultural practices such as flowing of plant residues into the soil (Muller, 1966, 1969; Putnam and Tang, 1986; Inderjit and Dakshini, 1992b, 1994a, 1995b and 1996).

The secondary metabolities such as Phenolics, alkaloids, polyacetylenes, fatty acids, and steroids – can be act as allelochemicals (Rice, 1984; Waller, 1987 and Inderjit *et al.*, 1995d). These chemicals are presents in various parts; however, their mere presence does not establish allelopathy (Putnam and Tang, 1986 and Heisey, 1990). To demonstrate their involvement in allelopathy, it is important to establish their direct release or indirect origin from plant derived materials in the environment and that the chemicals are present in sufficient quantities and persists for a sufficient time in the soil to affect plant species or microbes (Putnam and Tang, 1986). The overwhelming evidence indicates that phenolics do play a significant role in allelopathy. Phenolics have been implicated as having a role in allelopathic interactions among different group of plant such as Algae, Fungi, Lichens, Bryophytes, Pteridophytes, Gymnosperms, and Angiosperms (Rice, 1979; Fisher, 1987; Inderjit and Dakshini, 1994 and Lawrey, 1995).

Many scientist doubt that allelopathy is a significant factor in plant-plant interactions because good evidence for this phenomenon has been hard to obtain. It is easy to show that extract or purified compound from one plant can inhibit the growth of other plants in laboratory experiments, but it has been very difficult to demonstrate that these compounds are present in the soil in sufficient concentration to inhibit growth. Furthermore, organic substances in the soil are often bound to soil particles and may be rapidly degraded by microbes (Dao, 1987). In spite of the lack of supporting evidence, allelopathy is currently of great interest because of its potential agricultural applications. Reduction in crop yields caused by weed or residues from the previous crop may in some cases be result of allelopathy. An exiting future prospect is the development of crop plants genetically engineered to be allelopathic to weeds.

BRIEF HISTORY OF ALLELOPATHY

Allelopathy is not a new subject, but terms used were different Theophrastus (ca. 300 B.C.E.), a student and successor to Aristotle, wrote about allelopathic reactions in his botanical works. He has been called the "father of Botany", and wrote of how chickpea "exhausts" the soil and destroys weeds. In 1 C.E., Gaius Plinius Secundus, also known as Pliny the Elder, a roman scholar and naturalist, wrote about how chick pea and barley "scorch up" cornland. He also mentioned that Walnut trees are toxic to other plants (Smith and Secoy, 1977). De Candole (1832) suggested that some plants excrete some substances from their roots, which are harmful to other plants. He noted the specific inhibition of Oat by thistles (*Cirsium*), flax by Euphorbs (*Euphorbia*) and *Scabiosa* and wheat by rye (*Lolium*) plants. Most of the progress in this field occurred in the 19th century, farmers in America reported the loss of fertility in certain soils due to continued cropping of one crop over a long period and this lead to a revival of interest in excreted toxic substances. In early part of this century, Schreiner and his associates presented evidence that exhaustion of soil by single cropping is due to addition of growth inhibitors to the soils by certain crop plants (Schreiner and Reed, 1907a & b; Schreiner and Shorey, 1909; Schreiner and Sullivan, 1909; Schreiner and Lathrob, 1911). Since the 1960's allelopathy has been increasingly recognized as an important ecological mechanism which influences plant dominance, succession, formation of plant communities climax vegetation and crop productivity. It has been related to the problems with weed: Crop interference (Bell and Koeppe, 1972), Phytotoxicity in stubble mulch farming (McCalla and Haskins, 1964) and in certain type of crop rotations (Cornard, 1927). Rice (1984) indicated that allelopathy contributed to weed seed longevity problem through two mechanisms, (a) chemical inhibitors in the seed prevented their decay by microbes and (b) the inhibitors kept the seed dormant, although viable for many years.

The past reviews on allelopathy (Altieri and Doll, 1978; Bhandari and Sen, 1983; Lovett, 1983b; Rice, 1984, 1985; Putnam, 1985, 1986; Waller, 1987 and Einhellig and Leather, 1988) have dealt with grasslands, forestry and weeds. Some of these reviews slightly mentioned the crop production but none dealt exclusively with these important aspects. However, the indications of allelopathy had been observed in crop science. The phenomenon of allelopathy has received increasing attention within the past few decades particularly in relation to its significance in both natural and man managed ecosystems. Even so, several major difficulties have plagued research efforts in this area. Among these are lacks of agreement in nomenclature to define plant responses adequately, lack of reliable techniques to separate to prove the existence of direct vs. indirect influences via intermediate organisms (Putnam and Duke, 1978). Several workers have documented the existence of inhibitors in higher plants and microorganisms. They are found in aerial or underground plant parts or both causing allelopathic effects in a wide range of climate and plant communities. Plant parts known to contain inhibitors (Rice, 1974) are:

1. **Roots and Rhizomes:** In general, they have been found to posses fewer and less potent or smaller amounts of inhibitors than leaves, but sometimes it may be reverse also.
2. **Stem:** They are known to contain toxins, and in some cases stems are principal source of toxicity.
3. **Leaves:** They constitute the most consistent source of inhibitors. Many workers have demonstrated specific inhibitors in leaves.
4. **Flowers or inflorescence:** Although, study on flowers or inflorescence is limited, there is growing evidence that these organs bear high concentrations of inhibitors.
5. **Fruits:** Many fruits are known to content toxins and have inhibitory to microbial growth and seed germination.
6. **Seeds:** Seeds of many families and species have been found to inhibit seed germination and microbial growth.

The production of phytotoxin substances and their potentiality in allelopathy is of utmost importance. Substances producing allelopathic effects are virtually universal in the plant world (Datta and Sinha-Roy, 1983).

Allelochemicals substances produced by plants and are released from the plants by four general routs.

1. **Weathering:** Leaves and other plant parts falling on the ground may be decomposed by weathering and soil micro-organisms releasing various phytochemicals which may affect nearby species directly or indirectly (Rice, 1964 and Overland, 1966).
2. **Leaching:** Undoubtedly, plants are leaky systems when alive and more so when no longer living (Rice, 1974). Vast quantities of metabolites are emitted from the above ground parts of plants by the action of rain, fog or dew (Turkey, 1966). Leaching is a downward movement of a substance in a solution through the soil. Rain leaches the inhibitors, which remain in the soil, causing inhibition to germination.
3. **Exudation:** Metabolites are liberated from roots (Woods, 1960 and Rovira, 1969) and underground organs into the surrounding rhizosphere.
4. **Volatilization:** Volatile toxins from the plants escape into the environment (Muller, 1966). Because of their volatilizing property and affect the growth of other plants growing nearby.

Considerable evidences have been gathered during the past few decades, demonstrating the presence of inhibitory materials in a wide range of plant extracts and volatiles causing varying degree of inhibition. But the evidence concerning chemical nature of inhibitors or phytotoxins is insufficient. Moreover, it is not certain whether specific compounds are involved. Most chemical inhibitors are compounds, which belong to be class of secondary substances (Fraenkel, 1959 and Whittaker and Fenny, 1971). Since they occur sporadically, they have no apparent role in the basic metabolism of an organism with few exceptions, the secondary compounds can be grouped into five major categories namely, phenylpropenes, acetogenins, terpenoids, steroids and alkaloids.

Chemical nature of allelopathic compounds: There are thousands of compounds produce as secondary metabolites of plants. The categories of allelopathic agents reviewed by Rice (1984) in his book 'Allelopathy' are:

1. **Water-soluble simple organic acids:** Malic, citric, tartaric acid, acetaldehyde, malonic acid, fumaric acid, propionic acid, acetic acid and butyric acid. (Rice, 1984).
2. **Simple unsaturated lactones:** Parasorbic acid, protoanemonin are inhibitory to seed germination and are antibacterial (antibiotics such as patulin and penicillic acid are simple lactones and are antagonistic to microorganisms). (Rice, 1984).
3. **Long-chain fatty acids and Polyacetylenes:** Fatty acids, viz. myritic, palmitic, linolelaidic, oleic, stearic, arachidic, 11, 14-eicisadienoic, heneicosanic and behenic acids. Polyacetylenes are largely found on the plants of Acteraceae family. α-terthienyl, phenylheptatrine, safynol and dehydrosafynol. And diatretyne nitrile, diatretyne amide and diatretyne 3 from *Leucopaxillus* mycorrhizal fungus etc. are antimicrobial (Rice, 1984).
4. **Napthoquinones, Anthroquinones and complex quinines:** Juglone (5-hydroxynapthoquinone), Novarubin and 'Auremycin' (dimeric quinone) (Rice, 1984).
5. **Simple phenols, benzoic acid and derivatives, Phloroglucinol and polyphlorogluicinols:** Phenolics like vanillin, vanillic acid, hydroquinone, phloroglucinol and *p*-hydroxybenzoic acid. *p*-hydroxybenzoic and vanillic acid are commonly found benzoic acid derivatives in soil. Syringic acid in soil (corn field); gallic acid from *Euphorbia* spp.; gentistic acid (2,5-dihydroxybenzoic acid) by *Celtis*, sulfosalicylic acid (2-hydroxy-5-sulfobenzoic acid) by crab grass, phenolcarbonic acid from roots of tomato, polyphloroglucinols from brown algae (Rice, 1984).
6. **Cinnamic acid derivatives:** Derived from phenylalanine or tyrosine through Shikimic acid pathway, widespread in higher plants. Cinnamic, *o*-coumaric and *o*-hydrocoumaric, trans-cinnamic, chlorogenic and caffeic, ferulic acid, *p*-coumaric, chlorogenic, isochlorogwine, *p*-coumarylquinic acids etc. (Rice, 1984).
7. **Coumarins:** Lactones of *o*-hydroxycinnamic acid, Coumarin, esculetin, esculin, scopolin, furanocoumarins, psoralen, byakangelicin, isopimpinellin, bergapten, isobergapten, angelicin, xanthotoxin etc. (Rice, 1984).
8. **Flavonoids:** These are widespread in plants, quercetin, cyandin chloride, phloretin, catechin, diosmetin trioside, myricetin, isoflavonoids etc. (Rice, 1984).

9. **Hydrolysable and Condensed tannins:** Common hydrolysable tannin is a sugar ester of gallic acid; plant residues often contain ellagic chebulic, digallic, trigallic hexaoxyphenic acids etc are produced by hydrolysis of different tannins. Benoit and Starkey's (1968b) c.f. Rice (1984) worked on the condensed tannins that markedly inhibit the rate of decomposition of organic matter in soil (Rice, 1984).

10. **Terpenoids and Steroids:** These contain isoprene or isopentane units; basic terpenoids are monoterpenoids, sesquiterpenoids, diterpenoids, triterpenoids and tetratepenoids. Camphene, camphor, cineole, dipentene, α-pinene and β-pinene (from *Salvia* spp). Camphor and cineole terpenes are more toxic. Steroids like Digitoxigenin and Strophanthidin are strongly antimicrobial. (Rice, 1984).

11. **Amino acids and polypeptides:** Free amino acids from *Abutilon theophrasti* Medic. inhibit germination of several crops, unspecified amino acids are excuded by roots of Cucumber and tomato are phytotoxins, unusual amino acids act as antimetabolites in protein synthesis. Lycomarasmin polypeptides are produced by *Fusarium oxysporium* Schl., victorin by *Helminthosporium victoriae* Meehan & Murphy. and carbtoxinine by *H.carbonum* Ullstrup. and colletotin by *Colletotrichum* spp. (Rice, 1984).

12. **Alkaloids and Cyanohydrins:** Both are derived from amino acids. Alkaloids e.g. Caffeine, quinine, strychnine, berberine, cordeine, cinchonin, cinchonidin, tropa acid are strong inhibitors of germination. Other examples are: papaverine, ephedrine, piperine, atropine, esters of fusaric acid and α-picolinic acid etc. Cyanohydrins include 'Dhurrin' (from seedlings of *Sorghum bicolor* (L).Moench.) when hydrolyzed produce HCN, *p*-hydroxybenzaldehyde which are phytotoxic, amygdalin produce HCN and benzaldehyde that are toxic. (Rice, 1984).

13. **Sulphides and Mustard oil glycosides:** Allicin, a disulfide is produced from alliin is antibacterial (present in crushed garlic). Allyl isothiocyanate and allyl thiocyanate are produced from singrin (mustard oil glycosides). (Rice, 1984).

14. **Purines and Nucleosides:** There are several naturally occurring purines and nucleosides in plants in addition to those that are involved in nucleic acids. Examples: Caffeine, theophylline, paraxanthine, theobromine from coffee plants, antibiotics (nucleosides) like nebularine, cordycepin and nucleocidin etc. (Rice, 1984).

There are many other miscellaneous phytotoxins, e.g. Phenylacetic and 4-phenylbutyric acids; Phenethyl alcohol, Tryptophol, Ethylene etc. (Rice, 1984). Plants do not produce allelochemicals at all times. Some are present at all times while some are produced after injuries or infection by pathogens. Plants protect themselves against herbivores and pathogens by producing defense chemicals (Poisons) but face a problem of 'autotoxicity' (c. f. Khose, 2006). The alleochemicals released in the surrounding environment may affect other organisms in different ways. They affect internal as well as external morphology, growth and physiological process such as uptake of nutrients, photosynthesis, respiration etc.

SCOPE AND FUTURE STRATEGIES:

Allelopathy offers a great scope to reduce the ill-effects of modern agriculture practices such as present pesticides causes environmental pollution, contamination of drinking water resources, human and animal health hazards, residues in food chain and development of pesticides resistant/ tolerant species of pests in agroecosystems. These may be overcome using allelopathic strategies, hence it provides basis to sustainable agriculture and maintenance of clean environment for our future generations. Allelopathy can be used in multidisciplinary areas of research. Currently allelopathy research is being conducted in several fields of Agricultural and Biological sciences viz. Agroforestry and Forestry, Agronomy, Biochemistry, Biotechnology, Botany, Chemistry, Ecology, Entomology, Fresh Water Biology, Genetics and Plant Breeding, Horticulture, Limnology, Microbiology, Nematology, Plant Pathology, Soil Science, Vegetable Crops, Zoology etc. As traditional methods of discovering and developing new herbicides become more difficult and expensive, the interest in natural products as sources of herbicides chemistries have increased because of allelochemicals present in plant. Besides, public awareness and demand for environmentally safer herbicides with less persistence, more specific targets and less potential for contaminating ground water makes searches for new weed control strategies using natural products more attractive. Plants and microorganisms produce hundreds and thousands of secondary compounds. Many of these compounds are phytotoxic and have potential as herbicides or as templates for new herbicides classes. It has been estimated that only 30% of a possible 400,000 secondary metabolites from plants and microorganisms have isolated and identified. Only the fraction of those identified have been evaluated for herbicidal and bio regulator activity (Dodge, 1987 and Einhellig and Leather, 1988). These allelochemicals offer great potential for pesticides because they are free from problems associated with present pesticides. Therefore, allelochemicals are current areas of research for development of new pesticides (herbicides, insecticides, nematocides, fungicides). These could be used for weed control directly or their chemistry could be used to develop new herbicides. Most of the research in allelopathy has been done during the last three decades (1960 onwards) and quantum of research is increasing. It is hoped that till the end of twentieth century, allelopathy may be used in various forms to increase crop productivity. Recent developments:

a. In isolation, characterization, identification techniques of allelochemicals.
b. New techniques in biotechnology.
c. Use of allelochemicals to control pests (weeds, insects, nematocides, diseases) and to stimulate crop growth and yield.
d. New weed control practices using allelopathic crops may help in achieving this goal.
e. Useful in agriculture to increase yield.
f. Minimize some problems related to multiple cropping systems and
g. Soil productivity and availability of nutrients in soil.

Allelopathy is very young field of science; therefore research may be continued in all areas investigated in the past, allelopathic research will establish a boon in agricultural and forestry production (Narwal, 1994).

STUDY AREA: For the present study Pune district (Maharashtra State, India.) was selected as a study area, which comprises 14 Tahasils. As Pune is a well known for educational and industrial town located at the foot hills of Sahyadri Mountains at an altitude of 560 meters, with an area of 170.56 Sq.km. accommodating a population of 17,06,253. It is located at $73^0.51'$ in East longitude and $18^0.32'$ North latitude. The annual rainfall is 116.35 c.m. and the average Relative Humidity is 50% to 75%. The average temperature during summer 37^0C to 23^0C and during winter 30^0C-12^0C. Pune experiences the monsoon type of climate with a rainy, summer and dry winter period. Due to its location in the rain shadow region of Sahyadri range, where rainfall decreases towards the east, April and May are the hottest months, while December to January are the coldest months. Climatologically the district is broadly divided into two zones viz. rain fid zone and rain shadow zone. The rain shadow Tahasils lies in drought prone tract. This zone falls in the category of hot semiarid region. Due to this reason, the weed flora is rich in these Tahasils.

Thus for the present investigation preliminary surveys were carried out to find some medicinally important and allelopathic plants found to be growing in various agricultural fields of Pune district. These medicinal and allelopathic plants obviously are not found to be growing at any one place. Therefore, frequent visits were organized for the collection of plants growing in a particular area at a particular season of a year. Almost majority of plants are found to be growing either in association with crop plants or on the fallow lands, especially along roadsides and dumped fields. However, the plants which do not allow other plant species to grow near by and show their dominance were selected for the present investigation. In the present investigation, total four plants of family Cucurbitaceae were selected which are having both medicinal as well as allelopathic properties. These are as fallows:

1. *Citrullus colocynthis* **Schrader.**
2. *Coccinia grandis* **(Linn.) Voight.**
3. *Cucumis trigonus* **Roxb.**
4. *Diplocyclos palmatus* **(L.) C. Jeffery.**

These plants were collected in the months of October, November, December and January in large quantities from various fields of Pune district especially in the Tahasils like Pune, Haveli, Purandhar, Daund, Mulshi and Maval. (Plate No. I)

PLATE- I

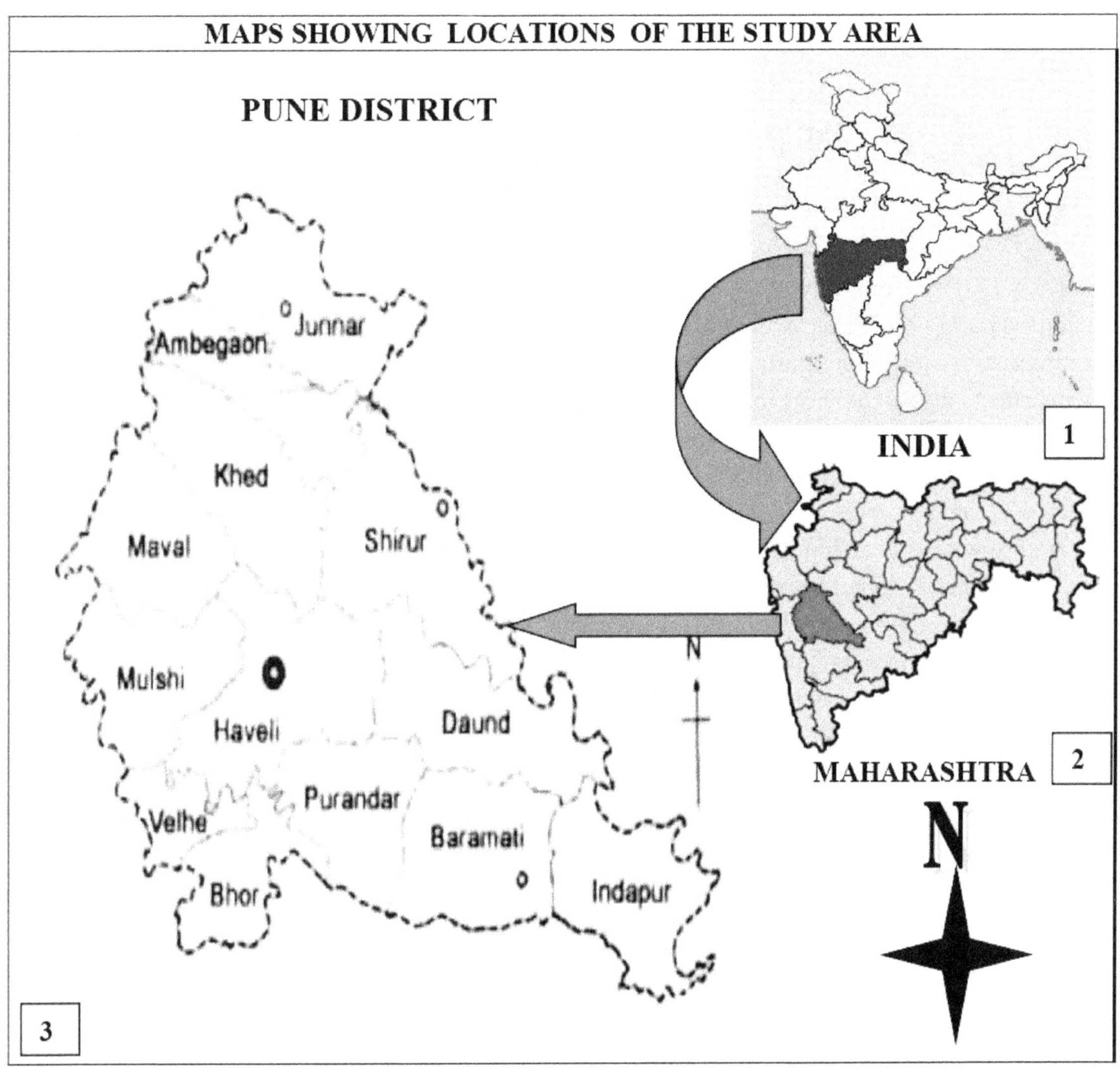

FIG. NO.1: MAP OF INDIA.
FIG. NO.2: MAP OF MAHARSAHTRA STATE.
FIG. NO.3: MAP OF PUNE DISTRCT.

CHAPTER TWO

Observations & Descriptions

Family Cucurbitaceae is commonly known as melons and watermelons which includes crops like cucumbers, squashes including pumpkins, luffas, gourds or cucurbits. It is a major family for economically important species. The family is predominantly distributed around the tropics, particularly where those with edible fruits. Some of these represent the earliest cultivated plants in both the Old and New Worlds. Majority of these are used as medicinal and economical purposes. The family is distinct morphologically and biochemically from other families and is therefore considered monophyletic. Most of the plants in this family are annual vines but there are also woody lianas, thorny shrubs and trees (*Dendrosicyos*). Many species have large showy, yellow or white flowers. Usually the stems are hairy, rough and angular. Stem tendrils are present at 90° to the leaf petioles at nodes. Leaves are exstipulate, alternate, simple, palmately lobed or palmately compound. The flowers are unisexual, usually dioecious, very rarely monoecious. The female flowers have inferior ovaries. The fruit is a kind of berry termed as pepo. There are about 125 extant genera in Cucurbitaceae, including 825 species.

In the present investigation, preliminary surveys were carried out to find out some medicinally important and allelopathic plants found to be growing in various agricultural fields of selected study area. However, the plants which do not allow other plant species to grow near their vicinity and were also expressed their dominance in the study area were selected for the present investigation. The following four members of Cucurbitaceae family were selected.

1. *Citrullus colocynthis* Schrader.
2. *Coccinia grandis* (Linn.) Voight.
3. *Cucumis trigonus* Roxb.
4. *Diplocyclos palmatus* (L.) C. Jeffrey.

1) *Citrullus colocynthis* **Schrader.** (Plate II: Figs. 4,5 & 6) The colocynth, also known as bitter apple in English, indrayan in Hindi and kadu-indravani in Marathi. It is a native of dry areas of North Africa. It is common weed found to be widely wild growing in the sandy lands of North West, the Punjab, Sind, Central and Southern India and on the Coromandal coast. Colocynth is not systematically grown anywhere in India, (Nadkarni, 2002). It has been known since Biblical times and cultivated in the Mediterranean region, especially in Cyprus and in India for many centuries. Its original scientific name was *Colocynthis citrullus*, but now it is named as *Citrullus colocynthis*. It is an annual plant resembling to the common watermelon. The stems are herbaceous and beset with rough hairs. The leaves stand alternately on long petioles. These are triangular, many cleft, variously sinuated, obtuse and hairy. It is a fine green on upper surface while rough and pale lower surface. Flowers are axillary solitary and yellow usually born at the axils of leaf. Fruit is globular, yellow and smooth, when ripe and contains white spongy pulp within a hard coriaceous rind along with numerous ovate compressed white or brownish seeds (Cooke, 1958). The pulp contains Colocynthin, a fixed oil, a resinous substance, gum, pectic acid or pectin, calcium and magnesium phosphates, lignin and water.

Medicinal and Other Uses: In pre-modern medicine it was an ingredient in the electuary called *confectio hamech* or diacatholicon. This is used in laxative pills. It is one of the most violent purgative drugs. Sometimes, it was taken with boiled water, or beer, in obstruction of the menses. Some women used it in the same manner, in the beginning of pregnancy, to cause an abortion. The mixture of unripe fruit of acacia; colocynth; dates; triturate with $6/7^{th}$ pint of honey is taken to stop pregnancy of woman. It is usually administered in the first, second or third period.

Moisten a pessary of plant fiber and place in the vagina (Riddle, 1999). The powder of colocynth was sometimes used externally with aloes, in unguents, plasters etc with remarkable success against parasitic worms. The same mixture is recommended as an enema. Remedies for counteracting colocynth have included emetics, such as zinc sulfate and apomorphine, if caught early; later, demulcents and opiates, with stimulants to combat collapse. It is a powerful hepatic stimulant and hydragogue cathartic. It is used as a strong laxative (Davis, 1909). Its seed is edible though bitter, nutty-flavored, and rich in fat and protein, is eaten whole or used as an oilseed. It is a traditional food plant in Africa. It has potential nutritional value hence, it is used as boost food security, foster rural development and support sustainable landcare (National Research Council, 2006). In Iran *C.colocynthis* is known by name *Shahm-e-Hanzal*. Its juice is used to make paper to protect the damage from mice and insects. It is used as an insecticides (Mehrnaz, 2008). The mosquito larvicidal activity was found in whole plant Petroleum ether extract of *C.colocynthis* (Abdul, 2008). Mullai and Jebanesan in 2007 tried the Petroleum ether and methonal extract of *C.colocynthis* for larvicidal, ovicidal and repellent activities. The fruit is used in Morocco for the purpose of protecting woolen clothing from moths (Hooker and Ball, 1878).

PLATE II
Citrullus colocynthis **Schrader.**

Fig. No.4: Habit of *Citrullus colocynthis* Schrader.

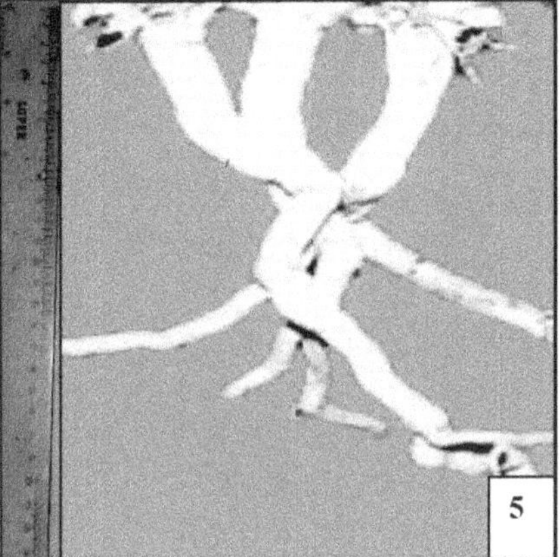

Fig. No.6: Flowering Twig of *Citrullus colocynthis* Schrader.

Fig. No.5: Root of *Citrullus colocynthis* Schrader.

2) *Coccinia grandis* (**Linn.**) **Voight.** (Plate III: Figs. 7, 8 & 9) It is a diocieous creeper found to be growing everywhere in hedges of India. In English it is known as Ivy gourd, Bimb in Hindi and Tondili in Marathi. It is a

perennial, tuberous rooted, climber with simple tendrils. Leaves are palmately 5-lobed with cordate base. Flowers are white. Fruits are fusiform and ellipsoid, slightly beaked, marked when immature with white streaks and bright scarlet when fully ripe. Seeds are somewhat obovoid and rounded at the apex. These are slightly papillose, much compressed and yellow-grey. It is wild on hedges everywhere on Deccan plateau, Gujarat, Bombay, Sind, Bengal, distributed throughout India and Tropical Africa (Cooke, 1958).

Medicinal and Other uses: Almost all plants parts (leaves, root, fruit and bark) are medicinally useful. The wild variety is bitter but cultivated variety is sweet. The fruits are edible used as a vegetable. Root contains resin, alkaloid, starch, sugar, gum, fatty matters, organic acid and ash. Glucokenin has the property of reducing the amount of sugar in the blood. The expressed juice taken from the crushed plant, when analysed was found to contain an enzyme, a harmone and traces of an alkaloid. Dried bark is a good cathartic. Leaves and stem are antispasmodic and expectorant. The plant has the reputation in Bengal of having a remarkable effect in reducing the amount of sugar in the urine of patients suffering from diabetes mellitus. Fresh expressed juice from the tuberous roots, stem and leaves is given either by itself or in combination with certain metallic preparations in early cases of diabetes such as pityriasis. Leaves are mixed with ghee and are applied like liniment to sores and skin diseases. Leaves are also applied to skin eruptions such as those of small-pox. The plant is generally used as tincture internally in gonorrhoea. Fresh juice of leaves is applied to the bites of animals; also applied to the body to induce perspiration in fevers. Green fruit is chewed to cure sores on the tongue. The ripe fruit is eaten raw as a vegetable, but is never given to children as it is supposed to blunt the faculties. Decoction of the leaves and stem is useful in bronchial catarrh and bronchitis. Leaves are boiled in gingelly oil and are applied to ringworm, psoriasis and itch. Oil is also used as an application to ulcers and as an injection into chronic sinuses (Nadkarni, 2002).

PLATE III
Coccinia grandis (Linn.) Voight.

Fig. No.7: **Habit of** *Coccinia grandis* (Linn.) Voight.

Fig. No.9: **Flowering Twig of** *Coccinia grandis* (Linn.) Voight.	Fig. No.8: **Root of** *Coccinia grandis* (Linn.) Voight.

3) *Cucumis trigonus* Roxb. (Plate IV: Figs. 10, 11 &12) It is known as a Bitter gourd in English, Bislambi in Hindi and Karit in Marathi. It is perennial, scabrid, monocecious. The stems are slender, angled and rough, clothed with short hairs. Stem tendrils are simple. Leaves are suborbicular in outline, 1-2 in. long and broad, scabrid on both surfaces, hispid on the nerves beneath, cordate at the base, deeply palmately 5-7 lobed. Flowers are yellow in colour. Fruit are ellipsoid or subglobose, longitudinally variegated with 10 green stripes while pale yellow when ripe, with bitter pulp. Seeds are white, ellipsoid and not marginated (Cooke, 1958).

Medicinal and Other Uses: There are two distinct varieties of these plants viz. the wild bitter *Pahadi Indrayan* and hill colocynth which is having smooth fruits with green and yellow streaks like colocynth. Fruit is appetizer, useful in bilious disorders. Wild bitter fruits are never eaten, but are used sometimes medicinally. Seeds are cooling and are beaten into a paste with the juice of *Cynodon dactylon* and applied to herpatic eruptions. In Malabar the plant is supposed to be alexipharmic and to have the power of removing pains and aches. Fruits are pounded and boiled with cow's milk and applied to the head to prevent insanity, strengthen the memory and remove vertigo. A decoction of the root is used as a purgative. It is stated to be milder in effect than the pulp of the fruit and causes less irritation. The drug is also used in shake-bite (Nadkarni, 2002). The major serine protease obtained from the fruit is used as a meat tenderizer. The enzymatic characteristics and N-terminal amino acid sequence of the purified protein indicated that it is a homologue of cucumisin (Mufti *et al.*, 2006).

PLATE IV
Cucumis trigonus Roxb.

Fig. No.10: Habit of *Cucumis trigonus* Roxb.

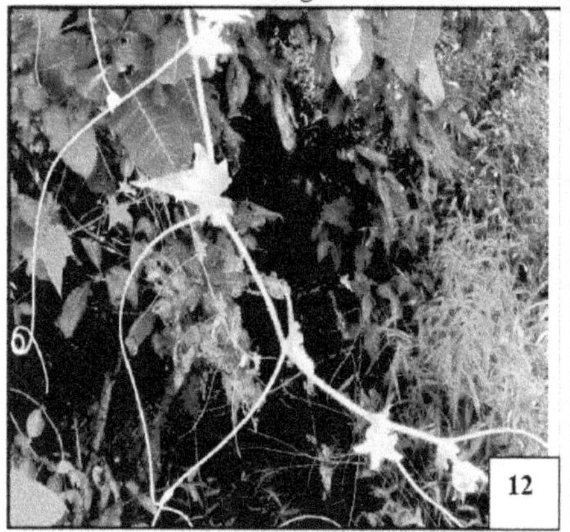

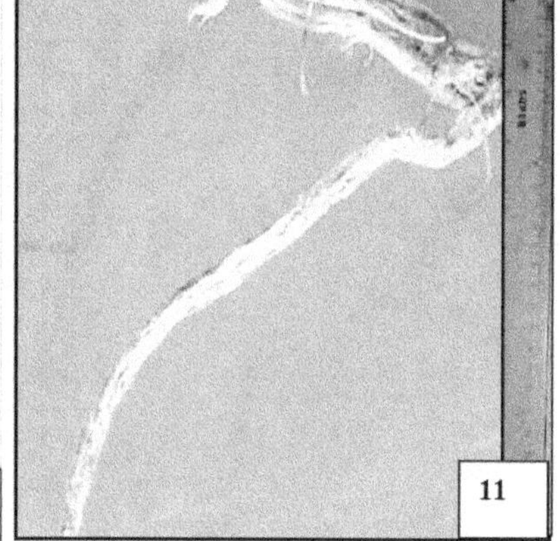

Fig. No.12: Flowering Twig of *Cucumis trigonus* Roxb.

Fig. No.11: Root of *Cucumis trigonus* Roxb.

4) *Diplocyclos palmatus* (L.) C. Jeffrey.(Plate V: Figs. 13, 14 & 15) It is known as Lollipop climber in English, Sivalingi in Hindi and in Marathi. Shivalingii. This plant is distributed throughout India, Tropical Africa and Australia growing wild, as a spreading plant. It is a perennial, monoecious herb climbing by bifid tendrils. Stems are upto 6 m long, young stems spotted with darker green. Leaves are alternate, simple; stipules absent; petiole 2–10 cm long; blade broadly ovate, palmately 5 lobed, up to 14 cm × 15 cm; base cordate; lobes narrowly elliptical or elliptical, margin sinuate-dentate. Inflorescence is an axillary cyme clusters with both male and female flowers in same axil. Flowers are unisexual, regular, 5-merous, corolla white to greenish-yellow; male flowers pedicellate, with 3 free stamens; female flowers subsessile, with inferior, 1-celled ovary, stigma 3-lobed. Fruit is subglobose, indehiscent berry 1.5–2.5 cm in diameter, solitary or clustered, red with silvery white longitudinal stripes; contain 1-2 small seeds. Looking like sivalinga (Cooke,1958).

Medicinal and Other Uses: Whole plant part is useful. It is used in vata, pitta and cough. It is also used in flatulence, skin diseases and general debility. The leaves are eaten as a vegetable in Kenya and in South-East Asia. Young fruits and shoots are occasionally eaten as well in South-East Asia. In Kenya the roots are used as an antivenin and fruits and leaves to cure stomach-ache. In Thailand stems are used as an expectorant and fruits as a laxative, and in Nepal seeds used as a febrifuge. The tribal people of Chhattisgarh used the seed of shivalingi, Sonth, Kalimirch, Putrajivi and root bark of Vat, is made in powder2-5gms. Powder is taken with water or milk at night, once daily for 21 days for curing Contraception (Shukla *et al.,* 2008).

PLATE V
Diplocyclos palmatus **(L.) C. Jeffery.**

Fig. No.13: Habit of *Diplocyclos palmatus* (L.) C. Jeffery.

Fig. No.15: Flowering Twig of *Diplocyclos palmatus* (L.) C. Jeffery.

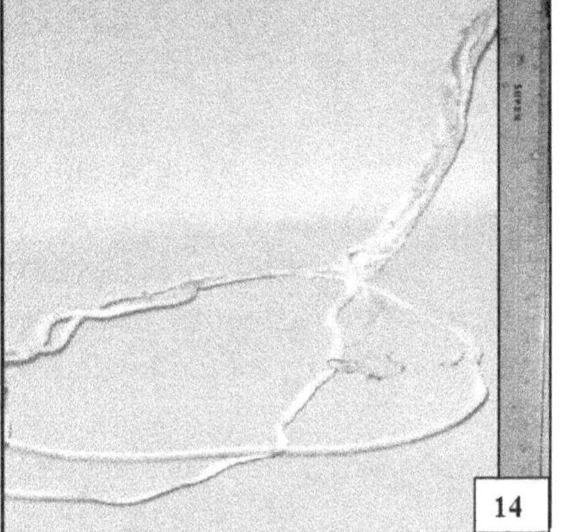

Fig. No.14: Root of *Diplocyclos palmatus* (L.) C. Jeffery.

CHAPTER THREE

Material and Methods

This topic is concerned with the methods and techniques used for the allelopathic study of some medicinally important plants species of family Cucurbitaceae. It is divided into five parts.

1) STUDY AREA AND PLANT COLLECTION:

For the present study Pune district (Maharashtra State, India.) was selected as a study area, which comprises 13 Tahasils. Pune experiences the monsoon type of climate with a rainy, summer and dry winter period. Due to its location in the rain shadow region of Sahyadri range, where rain fall decreases towards the east, which is receiving very scanty rainfall of about 0.0 – 8.0 cm. April and May are the hottest months, while December to January are comparatively coldest months. According to Sen (1982) this zone falls in the category of hot semiarid region. Thus, for the present investigation preliminary surveys were carried out to find some medicinally important and allelopathic plants found to be growing in various agricultural fields of Pune district. These medicinal and allelopathic plants obviously are not found to be growing at any one place. Therefore, frequent visits were organized for the collection of plants growing in a particular area at a particular season of a year. Almost majority of plants are found to be growing either in association with crop plants or on the fallow lands, especially at roadsides and dumped fields. However, the plants which do not allow other plant species to grow near by and show their dominance were selected for the present investigation. Finally, total four plants were selected having both medicinal as well as allelopathic properties.

The following four members of family Cucurbitaceae were selected.

1. *Citrullus colocynthis* **Schrader.**
2. *Coccinia grandis* **(Linn.) Voight.**
3. *Cucumis trigonus* **Roxb.**
4. *Diplocyclos palmatus* **(L.) C. Jeffery.**

These plants were collected in the months of October, November and December in large quantities from various fields of Pune district especially in the Tahasils like Pune, Haveli, Purandhar, Daund and Maval. At the same time natural photographs of these plants were taken in the field at different stages of their lifecycle. Efforts were made to collect these plants in flowering and fruiting conditions for the correct botanical identification. Collected plants were bought in the laboratory and correctly identified by using various floras, such as The Flora of the Presidency of Bombay (Cooke, 1958); Flora of India, (Hooker, 1894) and The Flora of Purandhar, (Santapau, 1957). These were further pressed, dried and finally herbarium sheet were prepared. The herbarium sheets were certified from the authorities of Botanical Survey of India (B.S.I.) Western circle, Pune and deposited in the Department of Botany, University of Pune for further reference. Usually healthy plants and their parts was collected, washed thoroughly, cleaned and further dried in the shade so as to prevent the decomposition of chemical constituents present in them and made into fine powders in blender.

2) LABORATORY BIOASSAY:

For all laboratory bioassays mature seeds of *Phaseolus aconitifolius* Jacq. variety – 'Abhaya'. were collected from agricultural shops (Seed suppliers). They were surface sterilized with 0.1% Mercuric chloride ($HgCl_2$) (w/v) solution followed by washing with sterilized distilled water for several times, carefully dried and used for examinations (bioassay) in terms of the inhibition of seed germination and seedling growth. The plant *Phaseolus aconitifolius* seeds was selected because its germination and seedling growth were very sensitive to all the extracts of selected plants species. To evaluate the allelopathic activity of *Cucumis trigonus, Citrullus colocynthis, Coccinia grandis* and *Diplocyclos palmatus* on *Phaseolus aconitifolius* seeds. Five types of bioassays were conducted in the laboratory.

A)Phytoextracts Bioassay:

To prepare phytoextracts healthy plants were collected from the different parts of agricultural fields as well as from barren waste lands where the plant species found to be growing abundantly. The collected plants were washed with distilled water to remove soil and dust particles. Phytoextracts were prepared in distilled water by crushing 100g of tissue of healthy and disease free parts of each plant containing root, stem and leaves in blender separately. The phytoextracts were filtered through Whatman No.1 filter paper and filtrates were brought to 250ml with addition of distilled water. These were served as inhibitor stock solutions (1:2.5) and used for bioassay.

Dilutions were made from the stock solutions (1%, 1.5%, 2%, and 2.5%). Surface sterilized 10 seeds of *Phaseolus aconitifolius* were placed in sterilized petridishes (11cm diameter) containing Whatman No.1 filter paper moistened with 10ml of phytoextracts of each plant of variable concentrations in separate petridishes. A petridishes containing Whatman No.1 filter paper moistened with 10ml distilled water served as control. Each petridish containing 10 seeds of *Phaseolus aconitifolius* were kept in triplicate at room temperature ($28 \pm 2^{\circ}C$). These petridishes were wrapped in brown paper so as to avoid direct sunlight. The emergence of radical was considered as the criterion for seed germination and was observed daily till 7 days and expressed as % seed germination. The observations of seed germination and simultaneously hypocotyl and radical length were measured after 7 days of sowing.

The phytoextracts bioassay consists of 3 types,

i. Root Extract Bioassay:

The selected plants roots were collected at different phonological phases from the fields. The fresh roots were washed with distilled water for 30 minutes to remove adhering soil particles. These fresh roots were crushed in blender. Phytoextracts of roots were prepared in distilled water by crushing 100g of tissues of roots. These phytoextracts were filtered through Whatman No.1 filter paper and filtrates were brought to 250ml with addition of distilled water. These were served as inhibitor solutions (1:2.5) and used for further bioassay. Five dilutions were made from the stock inhibitor solutions (1%, 1.5%, 2%, and 2.5% w/v). To determine the allelopathic effects of root phytoextracts of these plants, surface sterilized 10 seeds of *Phaseolus aconitifolius* were placed in sterilized petridish (11cm diameter) containing Whatman No.1 filter paper moistened with 10ml of root phytoextracts of each plant species of variable concentrations in separate petridish. A petridish containing Whatman No.1 filter paper moistened with 10ml distilled water served as control. Each petridish containing 10 seeds of *Phaseolus aconitifolius* were kept in triplicate at room temperature ($28 \pm 2^{\circ}C$). These petridishes were wrapped in brown paper so as to avoid direct sunlight. The emergence of radical was considered as the criterion for seed germination and was observed daily till 7 days and expressed as % seed germination. The observations of seed germination and simultaneously hypocotyl and radical length were measured after 7 days of sowing.

i. Stem Extract Bioassay:

For stem phytoextracts bioassay the fresh and healthy stem of each plant species were collected from different fields and brought to the laboratory. Then these stems were washed with distilled water so as to remove dust particles and unwanted debris. After cleaning with water the shoots of medicinal plants were chopped into small pieces in a grinder. Stem aqueous solutions of 1%, 1.5%, 2%, and 2.5% (w/v) five concentrations were prepared by dipping crushed stem materials of each species into 100ml of distilled water. The phytoextracts were then filtered through Whatman No.1 filter paper and used for bioassay.

In order to ascertain whether stem phytoextracts of selected plant species shows allelopathic effects on test crop, surface sterilized 10 seeds of *Phaseolus aconitifolius* were placed in sterilized petridish (11cm diameter) containing Whatman No.1 filter paper moistened with 10ml of stem phytoextracts of each plant species of variable concentrations in separate petridishes. A petridish containing Whatman No.1 filter paper moistened with 10ml distilled water served as control. Each petridish containing 10 seeds of *Phaseolus aconitifolius* were kept in triplicate at room temperature (28 ± 2^{0}C). These petridishes were wrapped by brown paper so as to avoid direct sunlight. The emergence of radical was considered as the criterion for seed germination and was observed daily till 7 days and expressed as % seed germination. The observations of seed germination and simultaneously hypocotyl and radical length were measured after 7 days of sowing.

iii. Leaf Extract Bioassay:-

For leaf extract bioassay the healthy and disease free leaves were separated from freshly collected above mentioned medicinal plants and washed with distilled water so as to remove soil and dust particles. After cleaning with water the leaves were chopped into small pieces in a grinder. Leaf aqueous solutions of 1%, 1.5%, 2%, and 2.5% (w/v). Five concentrations were prepared by dipping crushed leaf materials separately into 10ml of distilled water. The extracts were then filtered through Whatman No.1 filter paper and used for bioassay.

To find out effectiveness of inhibitors from leaf phytoextracts of all above plants on test crop, surface sterilized 10 seeds of *Phaseolus aconitifolius* were placed in sterilized petridish (11cm diameter) containing Whatman No.1 filter paper moistened with 10ml of leaf phytoextracts of each plant species of variable concentrations in separate petridishes. A petridish containing Whatman No.1 filter paper moistened with 10ml distilled water served as control. Each petridish containing 10 seeds of *Phaseolus aconitifolius* were kept in triplicate at room temperature (28 ± 2^{0}C). These petridishes were wrapped by brown paper so as to avoid direct sunlight. The emergence of radical was considered as the criterion for seed germination and was observed daily till 7 days and expressed as % seed germination. The observations of seed germination and simultaneously hypocotyl and radical length were measured after 7 days of sowing.

B) Leachates Bioassay:

Leachates are the removal of substances from plants by the action of aqueous solvents. Turkey (1962). All plants seem to be leachable, although the degree depends on type of tissue, stage of maturity and type, amount and duration of precipitation. Turkey (1962). A large diversity of allelopathic compounds are leached both organic and inorganic compounds such as phenolic acids, terpenoids and alkaloids. Turkey (1964).

The leachates bioassay consists of three types.

i. Root Leachates Bioassay: -

Fresh roots of 100g were taken from freshly collected healthy plants. These roots were washed in distilled water to remove soil particles. The roots were chopped into small pieces and were immersed in 100 ml distilled water and kept at room temperature (28 ± 2^{0}C) for 72 hrs. After 72 hrs the leachates was filtered through Whatman No.1 filter paper and the filtrate was used for bioassays, surface sterilized 10 seeds of *P. aconitifolius* were placed in sterilized petridishes (11cm. diameter) containing Whatman No. 1 filter paper, moistened with 10ml of root leachates solution were used for moistening filter paper. Each petridish containing 10 seeds of *P. aconitifolius* were kept in triplicate at room temperature (28 ± 2^{0}C). A petridish containing filter paper moistened with 10 ml distilled water served as control. These petridishes were wrapped by brown paper to avoid direct sunlight. The emergence of radical was considered as the criterion for seed germination and was observed daily till 7 days and expressed as % seed germination. The observations of seed germination and simultaneously hypocotyl and radical length were measured after 7 days of sowing.

ii. Stem Leachates Bioassay:-

For the preparation of stem Leachates 100g fresh stems of each plant species were taken from freshly collected healthy medicinal plant species. Then these stem were washed in distilled water to remove soil and dust particles. The stems were chopped into small pieces and were immersed in 100 ml distilled water and kept at room temperature (28 ± 2°C) for 72 hrs. After 72 hrs the leachates was filtered through Whatman No.1 filter paper and the filtrate was used for bioassays. Surface sterilized 10 seeds of *P. aconitifolius* were placed in sterilized petridishes (11cm. diameter) containing Whatman No. 1 filter paper, moistened with 10ml of stem leachates solution were used for moistening filter paper. Each petridish containing 10 seeds of *P. aconitifolius* were kept in triplicate at room temperature (28 ± 2°C). A petridish containing filter paper moistened with 10 ml distilled water served as control. These petridishes were wrapped by brown paper to avoid direct sunlight. The emergence of radical was considered as the criterion for seed germination and was observed daily till 7 days and expressed as % seed germination. The observations of seed germination and simultaneously hypocotyl and radical length were measured after 7 days of sowing.

iii. Leaf Leachates Bioassay:-

One hundred gram leaves of each plant species were separated from freshly collected plant species. Then these leaves were washed in distilled water to remove soil and dust particles. These leaves were immersed separately in 100 ml distilled water and kept at room temperature (28 ± 2°C) for 72 hrs. After 72 hrs the leachates was filtered through Whatman No.1 filter paper and the filtrate was used for bioassays. Surface sterilized 10 seeds of *P. aconitifolius* were placed in sterilized petridishes (11cm. diameter) containing Whatman No. 1 filter paper, moistened with 10ml of leaf leachates solution were used for moistening filter paper. Each petridish containing 10 seeds of *P. aconitifolius* were kept in triplicate at room temperature (28 ± 2°C). A petridish containing filter paper moistened with 10 ml distilled water served as control. These petridishes were wrapped by brown paper to avoid direct sunlight. The emergence of radical was considered as the criterion for seed germination and was observed daily till 7 days and expressed as % seed germination. The observations of seed germination and simultaneously hypocotyl and radical length were measured after 7 days of sowing.

C) Decomposition Bioassay:

The decomposition of plant residues potentially provides the largest quantity of allelochemicals that may be added to the rhizophore. After plant death, materials compartmentalized in cells are released and these processes with regard to allelopathy are the nature of the plant residues, the soil type and the conditions of decomposition. Patrick *et al.* (1964) reported that depending on the decomposing conditions, substances highly toxic, non-toxic or stimulatory to may be found during the decomposition of similar plant residues. In general more severe and persistant toxicity has been reported from cold and wet soil (McCalla and Haskins, 1964).

Since the decomposing plant materials are never equally distributed throughout the soil, the soil adjacent to the decomposing debris may contain more decomposition products than other areas. Therefore, as the roots grow through the soil, at same point they may come in contact with decomposing plant residues and are affected by allelochemicals. In decaying crop residues different types of allelochemicals differing in their activity are produced depending upon the organisms that digest them.

To judge the activity of the decaying plant parts, healthy plant parts of plant species were taken from freshly collected plants. These plants parts including leaves, stem and roots were dried in shade for 8 to 10 days. Then these plant parts were ground thoroughly and mixed with loamy soil (250g) at the rates of 2g, 4g, 8g, 16, and 32g and allow withering away for 40 days in the pots. The pots containing soil and grounded plant parts were kept wet by addition of equal amount of distilled water. The pots were periodically observed to ensure them to remain wet.

After 40 days of withering these mixtures were dried in air and placed in sterilized petridishes at the rates of 20g per petridish. These petridishes were lined with Whatman No.1 filter paper wetted with 10 ml of distilled water and surface sterilized 10 seeds of *Phaseolus aconitifolius* were kept in triplicate at room temperature (28 ± 2°C). A petridish containing 20g of soil free from decaying plant parts and Whatman No.1 filter paper wetted with 10 ml of distilled water served as control. All these petridishes were wrapped in brown paper so as to avoid direct sunlight. At the end of each experiment, the readings were recorded in the form of seed germination percentage and simultaneously hypocotyls and radicle length were measured after 7 days of sowing.

D) Volatilization Bioassay:

In few cases, allelochemicals may volatilize and absorbed directly from the atmosphere by neighboring plants and absorbed from condensate in dew, be absorbed on the soil particles and subsequently taken up by contact with plants or from the soil solution (Muller, 1966). Apparently several terpenoids transfer in these ways. Higher plants produce a variety of essential oils. From the plants rich in such compounds, these may be released continuously to the atmosphere. Usually this process enhances in hot weather, therefore, this phenomenon is observed in the arid regions of the world. Thus a number of species from several climatic regions may express allelopathy through volatilization (Rice, 1974 and Horsley, 1977). Muller (1966) reported that terpenes volatilizes by several species which inhibits the growth of near by plants.

To test volatile substance from the selected plant species, if any involved in the inhibitory effect on neighboring plants. Fresh plants were collected from different localities. All fresh parts of plant were cleaned with brush to remove soil and dust particles. From each plant species fresh parts (150g) were kept in surface sterilized air tight glass jar (Desicator) for 72 hrs. Soil (150 g.) and water (150 ml.) were kept inside the glass jar separately inside the jar in such a way that they were not in direct contact with the plant materials and the air inside only acts as a carrier for volatile substances. The soil and water, thus obtained were used for further bioassays using the crop. For laboratory bioassays 10 surface sterilized seeds of *Phaseolus aconitifolius* were placed in sterilized petridish (11cm) containing a Whatman No.1 filter paper. 10 ml water obtained from glass jar was utilized to moisten the filter paper, and 10 g soil obtained from glass jar was used as a layer of growth medium and made wet with distilled water. A petridish containing Whatman No. 1 filter paper moistened with 10 ml of distilled water and control soil (free from experimental plant) moistened with 10 ml of distilled water served as control. Data were recorded after 7 days. Each petridish containing 10 seeds of *Phaseolus aconitifolius* were kept in triplicate at room temperature ($28 \pm 2^{\circ}C$). All the petridishes were wrapped by brown paper so as to avoid direct sunlight.

The observations of seed germination and simultaneously hypocotyl and radicle length were measured after 7 days of sowing.

E) Root Zone Soil Bioassay:

The root exudates are those substances released from intact live plant roots into the surrounding medium (Rovira, 1969) although their volume is small i.e. 2-12% of the total gross photosynthates, but they play significant role in allelopathy (Woods, 1960; Rovira, 1969; Whittakar, 1971 and Rice, 1974). The root exudates are mediators in the interrelationship between higher plants and microorganisms. These root exudates are also important for the elimination of waste metabolic products from the plants (Grodzinsky, 1982). A variety of compounds are exuded from the roots which may influence the growth of microorganisms and associated higher plants.

In order to ascertain whether these plant species can show allelopathic effect through root exudation. Root zone soils, which had previously been heavily infested with the plants, were collected up to 3-4in depths. In the laboratory these soil samples were air dried, sieved through 0.5mm sieve, mesh screen and used for further bioassays. For laboratory bioassay 20g of each soil was taken in sterilized petridish (11cm) lined with single layer of Whatman No.1 filter paper. Surface sterilized 10 seeds of *Phaseolus aconitifolius* were placed in each petridish containing 20g soil and Whatman No. 1 filter paper. These petridishes were moistened with 10 ml of distilled water. Each petridish containing 10 seeds of *Phaseolus aconitifolius* were kept in triplicate at room temperature ($28 \pm 2^{\circ}C$). For comparison 20g of control soil (free from growth of experimental plants) were used. All the petridishes were wrapped by brown paper so as to avoid direct sunlight. Observations of seed germination and simultaneously hypocotyl and radicle length were measured after 7 days of sowing. To find out the effectiveness of inhibitors out from test species, and soil inhabited with these plants were analyzed to determine if these plants causes change in physical and chemical properties, which could account for the allelopathic effects.

Soil samples were collected at 3-4in depth from beneath the plant species stand. These samples were air dries, passed through 0.5mm sieve, and analysed for pH (Jackson, 1973), EC (Jackson, 1973 and Black, 1965), Organic Carbon (Black, 1965), Available Phosphorus (Bray and Kurtz, 1945), Available Potassium (Jackson, 1973), Available

Zinc (Zn), Copper (Cu), Iron (Fe) and Manganese (Mn)(Lindsay and Norvell, 1978).

3)ROOT ZONE SOIL ANALYSIS: -

Soil fertility plays an important role in increasing crop production in almost all soils of the world. Soil fertility is the quality that enables the soil to provide the proper nutrients in proper amount and in the proper balance, for the growth of specified crop plants. Soil fertility thus comprises not only in supply of nutrients but also their efficient management.

A soil testing thus provides an inventory of the plant nutrients and other chemical factors important for crop production. This inventory used as a basis for recommending additional nutrients in the form of fertilizers when required. The amount and kinds of nutrients recommended depends on the crop to be grown, the target yield and the amount of nutrients already present in the soil.

Phases of soil Analysis:

1. Collection of soil samples from root zones of selected plant weeds: Root zone soils, which had previously been infested with the plant weeds, were collected with the help of screw auger separately.

2. Analysis of the soil samples in the laboratory: These soil samples were air-dried, processed and analyzed for various physical and chemical properties.

All the soil samples collected beneath the roots of plant weeds were analysed in terms of pH, EC, Organic Carbon, available Phosphorus, Potassium, Zinc (Zn), Copper (Cu), Iron (Fe) and Manganese (Mn) by following methods.

1. Determination of soil pH: Perkin Elimer pH meter glass electrode 1:2.5 soil : water ratio (Jackson, 1973).

Principle: One of the enlightening attributes of a soil is its pH. Whether a soil acidic, or basic has much to do with the solubility of various components, the relative bonding of ions on exchange sites, and activity of various microorganisms. The plant nutrient availability is influenced by soil pH. The ideal pH range for availability of nutrients is 6.5 to 7.5.

Equipments required for soil pH:

The pH meter consists of two electrodes.

a. Glass electrode, and

b. Calomel electrode (reference electrode)

Reagents:

Standard buffer solution, pH 4.00:

Stock solution was prepared by using 0.3M potassium hydrogen phthalate by dissolving 15.3g of the analytical grade salt in about 225ml of hot water, cools down the solution, and dilutes it to 250ml. Add a drop of toluene to discourage growth of microorganisms. For the standard buffer pH 4.0 mix 100ml of the stock solution with 500ml distilled water.

a. Standard buffer solution, pH 9.2.

Dissolve 3.18g sodium tetra borate (A.R.) in distilled water and dilute to 1000ml.

b. 1.0 N. Potassium chloride solution (A.R.).

Apparatus:

Electrometric pH meter with glass and calomel electrodes.

Procedure:

a. Weigh 20g air dried soil into a beaker and add 50ml distilled water at regular intervals for one hour.

b. In the mean time turn the pH meter on , allow it to warm up, and standardize the glass electrode using both the standard buffers. Remember to adjust the temperature compensation knob to the temperature of the solution. Measure the pH of the sample suspension, stirring the suspension well just introducing the electrodes.

c. Rinse the electrodes after each determination and carefully blot them dry with filter paper before the next determination. Standardize the glass electrode after every ten determinations.

d. To determine pH in 1.0 N KCI use 50ml 1.0 N KCI instead of water. Stir at regular intervals for one hour. Let it settle and measure the pH of the clear supernatant solution.

2. Determination of Electrical conductivity of soil (EC): EC meter method (Jackon, 1973 & Black, 1965.)

Principle: The electrical conductivity of water extract of soil gives a measure of the soluble salt content of the soil. Pure water is a very poor conductor of electric current; whereas water containing dissolved salts ordinarily found soil conducts current approximately in proportion to the amount of soluble salts present. Based on this fact, the measurement of the electric conductivity of an extract gives a satisfactory indication of the total concentration of ionized constituents.

Measuring the electrical resistance between parallel electrodes immersed in the solution or soil extract makes the determination of electrical conductivity. In such a system, the solution between the electrodes becomes an electrical conductor to which the physical laws relating to resistance are applicable. The electrical resistance (R) is directly proportional to the distance (L) between the area (A) of the conductor. Thus $R = rL/A$, where 'r' is a proportionately constant known as the electrical resistivity, the value of which depends on the nature of conductor. If R is measured in ohms, L in cm and A in cm^2 the units of 'r' is ohm/cm.

Equipment:

a. Potassium chloride (KCL), 0.01 M:

Dissolve 0.7456g of KCL in distilled water, and add water to make the volume 1 Litre at 25^0c. This is a standard reference solution. At 25^0c, it has an electrical conductivity of 0.0014 Ohm/cm.

Procedure:

a. Weigh 20g air-dried soil into a 100ml beaker.
b. Add 50ml distilled water.
c. Stir at regular intervals for 1 hr.
d. Allow it to settle for 30 min and measure the conductivity by dipping the electrode in the supernatant.
e. To determine the cell constant, determine the conductivity by the 0.01M KCL solutions, and measure the temperature of the solution.
f. The cell constant K is given by,

Known conductivity of 0.01 M KCL

Cell constant (K) = Conductivity of 0.01 M KCL measured.

$Ece_{25} = Ec_T \times K \times F^t$

Where, Ece_{25} is the conductivity of the extract at 25^0c.

Ec_T is the apparent conductivity of the extract as measured.

K is the cell constant; F^t is the temperature correlation factor.

Now a day the temperature correlation is provided in the instrument itself.

3. Determination of Organic Carbon of soil: (Black, 1965)

Principle: Organic carbon content of soil organic matter comprises of 18 to 48 % of the total organic matter. Therefore, organic carbon determinations are often used as a basis for organic matter estimation though multiplying the organic carbon value by a factor. In this method the soil is digested with chromic acid and sulphuric acid making use of the heat of dilution of sulphuric acid. The excess of chromic acid not related by organic matter of the soil is determined by titration with standard ferrous sulphate solution. The importance of this method is that it gives an indication of the organic matter content of the soil, which is generally used as the index of soil fertility. The organic carbon content is multiplied by the factor 1.724 to obtain organic matter percentage. There is also a close relationship between the carbon and nitrogen of soil (C: N ratio). This method gives only approximate value because all the carbon, which is oxidized, is 60 to 90 % i.e. actually only about 75% of organic carbon is converted to CO_2. Therefore the necessary correction must be made in calculating the total carbon as well as the organic matter content of the soil.

Reagent:

i.   1N Potassium dichromate: Dissolve 49g Potassium dichromate in distilled water and dilute to 1lit. in volumetric reagent grade flask.

ii. 0.5 N Ferrous Ammonium Sulphate (F.A.S.): Dissolve 196.1g of F.A.S. in 300ml distilled water, add 20ml conc. Sulphuric acid dilute to 1lit.

iii. Diphenyl amine indicator: Dissolve 0.5g of Diphenylamine in 100ml of conc. Sulphuric acid.

iv. Phosphoric acid (85%) or Sodium fluoride.

v.   Concentrated Sulphuric acid: Concentration not less than 96% (sp. gr. 1.84)

Procedure:

Part A) Back Titration:

1.0g of soil (ground and sieved through 0.2mm) is placed in a dry 500ml conical flask. Add exactly 10ml of 1N potassium dichromate by means of pipette. Add 20ml conc. Sulphuric acid, shake the contents of the flask and keep aside on an asbestos sheet for 30min. Add 200ml water and 10ml of Phosphoric acid or 0.5g sodium fluoride and 1ml of Diphenylamine indicator. The content of the flask attain a bluish purple colour. Titrate this solution with 0.5N F.A.S. till the colour flashes to green. Note the reading as X ml.

Part B) Black Titration:

Pipette out 10ml of 1N Potassium dichromate in conical flask. Add 20ml conc. Sulphuric acid and 10ml Phosphoric acid and 1ml Diphenylamine indicator. Titrate with 0.5N F.A.S. solution till green colour is obtained. Note the reading as Y ml.

Calculations:

$K_2Cr_2O_7 + 4H_2SO_4 = K_2SO_4 + Cr_2(SO_4)_3 + 4H_2O + 3(O)$

$6FeSO_4 + 3H_2SO_4 + 3(O) = 3Fe_2(SO_2)_3 + 3H_2O.$

$3(C) + 6(O) = 3CO_2.$

i.e. Every molecule of $K_2Cr_2O_7$ gives out 3 atoms of nascent oxygen in presence of H_2SO_4 and three atoms of carbon will require six atoms of nascent oxygen for oxidation which will be released from two molecules of $K_2Cr_2O_7$.

Therefore, 2 molecules of $K_2Cr_2O_7 = 6(O) = 3C$.

2 x 294g of $K_2Cr_2O_7 = (12 \times 3)$g of Carbon.

Percentage of Organic Carbon = (Y-X) x N x 0.003 x 100 / wt. of soil x 4/3.

Where,

Y = ml of standard $FeSO_4$ or F.A.S required for blank.

X = ml of standard $FeSO_4$ or F.A.S. required for soil sample.

N = Normality of standard $FeSO_4$ solution or F.A.S. solution.

¾ factor is used because this method oxidizes about 75% of organic matter.

Percentage of organic matter - % Organic Carbon x 1.724.

Conclusion:

1. If the % Organic Carbon is less than 0.5- low.

2. If the % Organic Carbon is Less than 0.5 to 0.75- medium.

3. If the % Organic Carbon is more than 0.75-High.

4. Determination of Available Phosphorous from soil by Bray-II extractant with Spectrophotometer at 660um: (Bray and Kurtz, 1945)

Chlorostannous – reduced molybdophosphoric blue colour method in HCl system method is primarily meant for soils, which are moderately to strong acid (pH around 5.5 or less). In this, NH_4 F⁻ HCl combinatiopn is designation as measure of adsorbed plus.

Reagent:

1. NH_4 F⁻ HCl in 0.025 N HCl solution: Dissolve 2.775g of NH_4 F (AR) to 2.5 litres of 0.025 N HCl.

2. Ammonium molybdate solution: 15g of ammonium molybdate is dissolved in 300ml warm distilled water and filtered, if necessary, after cooling. To this, 350 ml of 10 n HCl is added and made up to 1 litre.

3. Stannous Chloride solution: Stock solution:- 10g of crystalline $SnCl_2$. $2H_2O$ is dissolved in 25ml of concentrated HCl by warming and stored in amber coloured bottle, carefully avoiding all contact with air. A piece of tin metal (AR) added will keep the stock solution for month.
4. Dilute solution: Working solution: 0.5 ml of $SnCl_2$ stock solution diluted to 66ml with distilled water. Prepare dilute solution fresh every time.
5. Boric acid, 0.8M: Dissolve 50g boric acid in water and volume is made up to 1 litre.
6. Standard P solution: Weigh 0.439g of KH_2PO_4 and dissolved in 50ml-distilled water + 25ml of 7N H_2SO_4 (Approx.) volume made up to 1 litre. This gives 100ppm stock solution (100ug P/ ml). Add 5 drops of toluene to diminish, microbial activity.
7. Working P solution: Take 20ml of stock solution of P (100ppm) in 1000ml volumetric flask and made up to the volume. This gives 2ug P/ml (2ppm). The normality of HCl should be adjusted correctly by titration.

Procedure:

1. Take 5g soil in 250ml conical flask.
2. Add to it 50ml of $NH_4 F^-$ HCl solution.
3. Shake the contents exactly for 5min. on platform type shaker.
4. Filter the contents immediately after shaking and collect the filtrate.

Estimation:

1. Pipette out 5ml $NH_4 F^-$ HCl extract into 25ml volumetric flask and to avoid interference of fluoride, and 7.5 ml of 0.8 M Boric acid, if necessary.
2. Add 5ml of ammonium molybdate solution.
3. Then neck of flask is washed drawn and the contents diluted to 22ml with distilled water and then add 1ml of dilute solution of $SnCl_2$ and volume made up to the mark.
4. Run the blank without soil.

The intensity of blue colour is measured at 660nm or 882nm using red filter just after 10min. The concentration of P determined from standard curve. This is very important as colour starts fading after some time.

Preparation of standard curve:

1. Prepare a series of standards by taking 0, 1, 2, 3, 4, 5 and 10ml of 2ppm P solution in 25ml volumetric flask respectively.
2. Add 5ml of $NH_4 F^-$ HCl reagent to each flask.
3. Add 5ml of ammonium molybdate.
4. Develop the colour and record the readings as above.
5. Construct graph by plotting readings on 'Y' axis and concentration of P on 'X' axis (i.e. ug P/ml).

Calculations:

Available P kg/ha = $R/10^9$ X Volume of 5ml extractant added / Aliquot taken x Final volume made 25ml X 2.24 X 10^6 X Weight of sampling 5ml 5g

To convert ug into Kg To convert g into Kg = R X 50/5 X 25 X 2.24/5 = R X 112

Where, R = ug P/ ml from standard curve

Interpretation of Results i.e. Rating

Class Available P Kg / ha., Very low 0-7, Low 7-14, Moderate 14-21, Moderately 21-28, High 28-35, Very high More than 35.

5. Determination of available Potassium from soil by flame Photometer method. (Jackson, 1973)

Principle: In flame photometer technique, the sample is aspired into a flame in the form of a spray. In flame, the solvent gets evaporated leaving the dehydrated salt behind. The salt is dissociated into free gaseous atoms in their ground state. Some of them ground level atoms take energy from flame and reach to their excited electronic state. The excited atom upon returning back to ground level state emits the radiation of characteristics wavelength. The emitted characteristics radiation can be measured with the help of monochromatic and a detector set up. In commonly used flame photometer, the specific filters are used for different elements, a monochromater who allows passing the wavelength specific to that particular element. The intensity of emitted radiation is always proportional to the concentration of the element in the flame, thus the calibration. The percentage of $CaCO_3$ of soil = -------% and therefore the soil is -----------. Curve can be prepared using various standards of the element. The flame photometric method is suitable for measuring the concentration of the element like, Na, K, and Ca because they may be excited to higher energy levels with low temperature ordinary gas flames. The term available potassium (K) conventionally refers to exchangeable + water soluble K. The exchangeable K constitutes the major portion of available K except in saline salts. Available K or exchangeable K is determined in the neutral normal ammonium acetate (1N NH_4OAC) extract of soil. Shaking followed by filtration or centrifugation carries out the extraction. The K estimated by using flame photometer.

Reagents:

1. 0N Ammonium acetate (pH 7.0): Dissolve 77.0gm of ammonium acetate (CH_3COONH_4) in water and dilute to 900ml & distilled. Mix thoroughly, Adjust pH to 7.0 with dilute NH4OH or acetic acid as required and make the final volume to 1 litre.
2. Standard potassium chloride solution: Make the stock solution of 1000 ppm of K by dissolving 1.908 g of AR grade potassium chloride is distilled water and up to 1 litre. Prepare 100-ppm standard by diluting 100ml of 1000ppm stock solution of K to 1 litre with the extracting solution.

Preparation of standard curve:

1. Pipette out 0,10,20,30 & 40 ml of 100-ppm solution into 100ml volumetric flask and the volume to the mark with extracting solution (in NH_4OAC solution). The solution contains 0, 10, 20, 30, and 40 ppm of K respectively. Add2 drops of n-butyl alcohol to each filtrate to improve its spraying properties.
2. Attach the appropriate filter and adjust the gas and air pressure.
3. Adjust the flame photometer at zero for the blank (ammonium acetate) and 100 for 40 ppm K.
4. Plot the graph of flame photometer reading against the different concentrations of Potassium.

Procedure:
Extraction:

1. Place 5g of soil in 100ml conical flask and 25ml neutral normal ammonium acetate (pH 7.0).
2. Shake for 5 minutes and immediately filter through Whatman No.1 filter paper. First few ml of the filtrate may be rejected.
3. Determine K in the extract from the flame photometer using K filter.
4. Find the K contents of the filtrate from the standard curve as K in kg / ha as follows.

Calculations:
Volume of extract 2.24 X 10^6
Available K = AX ___________________ X ______________ (Kg / ha) Weight of soil 10^6
=Appm X 25/5 X 2.24
Available K = Appm X 11.2 (Kg / ha)
Rating scale :- Available K -------- less than 150kg/ ha ---------low 150 – 250kg / ha ------------Medium

Greater than 250 kg/ ha-----High

Result: The soil contains---------- kg / ha available K. Therefore the soil has low/ medium / high available K.

6. Determination of Available Zinc (Zn), Copper (Cu), Iron (Fe) and Manganese (Mn). (Lindsay and Norvell, 1978).

Principle: Chelating agents offer great promise for assessing readily-available micronutrient cations in soils. These agents combine with free metal ions in solution to form soluble complexes. DTPA (Diethylene Triamine Penta Acetic Acid) offers a most favourable combination of stability constants for the simultaneous complexing of Zn, Cu, Mn, and Fe. To avoid excessive dissolution of $CaCo_3$ can release occluded micronutrients, the extractant is buffered in a slightly alkaline pH range and in part by including soluble Ca^{2+}. Triethanolamine (TEA) is used as buffer because it burns cleanly during atomization and has a pka = 7.8. At the selected pH of 7.3, three fourth of TEA is protonated and is present as $HTEA^+$. When the extractant is added to the soil, additional Ca^{2+} and some Mg^{2+} enter the solution, largely because the protonated TEA exchanges with Ca^{2+} and Mg^{2+} from soil exchange sites. This raises the concentration of ionic Ca^{2+} by two to three fold and aids in suppressing the dissolution of $CaCO_3$ in calcareous soils with a 2:1 solution to soil ratio. The capacity of DTPA to complex each of the micronutrient cations is 10 times its atomic weight and ranges from 550 to 650 ppm depending on the micronutrient cation. Thus DTPA is present in excess of the micronutrient metal cations that are normally solubilized during an extraction. This excess reduces the possibility that the extraction of one micronutrient might significantly affect the amount of other micronutrient extracted.

Reagents,

The following reagents are needed:

DTPA = 0.0005M (formula weight 393.35), $CaCl_2.2HO_2$ = 0.001M solution, TEA = 0.1 M solution.

Extracting Solution

To prepare 1 litre of DTPA extracting solution, dissolve 13.1 ml reagent grade TEA, 1.967g DTPA (AR grade) and 1.47g of $CaCl_2$ in 100ml of glass distilled water. Allow sometimes for the DTPA to dissolve and dilute to approximately 900 ml. Adjust the pH to 7.3$\pm$ .05 with 1:1 HCL while stirring and dilute to 1 litre. Addition of approximately 4ml of 1N HCL will bring the pH of the solution to 7.3. This solution is stable for several months.

Standard Solutions

Zinc Standard Solution: Dissolve 0.439g AR grade $ZnSO_4$. $7H_2O$ in 200ml of glass distilled water in a beaker. Add 5ml of 1:5 H_2SO_4. Transfer to a litre measuring flask and make volume to the mark to have a standard solution of 100ug Zn/ml (100ppm). Transfer 10ml of this standard to 100ml volumetric flask and dilute to the mark with DTPA extracting solution to have stock solution of 10ug Zn/ml (10ppm). For preparing working standards, transfer1,2,4 and 6ml of stock solution (10 ug Zn/ml) to a series of clean 100ml volumetric flasks and dilute each to the mark with DTPA extracting solution.

Volume of stock Zn solution taken : 0 1 2 4 6ml

Concentration of Zn now in solution:0 0.1 0.2 0.4 0.6ug/ml (ppm)

Iron Standard Solution: Dissolve 0.702 g of AR grade ammonium ferrous sulphate $(NH_4)_2SO_4FeSO_4.6H_2O$ IN 300ml deionized or glass distilled water in a beaker. Add 5ml of 1:5 H_2SO_4. Transfer to a litre measuring flask and make volume to the mark to have a standard solution of 100ug Fe/ml (100ppm). To prepare working standards, transfer1,2,4 and 6ml of stock solution and dilute each to the mark with DTPA extracting solution

Volume of stock Fe solution taken : 0 1 2 4 6ml

Concentration of Fe in solution : 0 1 2 4 6ug/ml (ppm)

Manganese Standard Solution: Dissolve 0.288g potassium permanganate $(KMnO_4)$ AR grade in 300ml deionized water in a beaker. Add 20ml concentrated H_2SO_4, warm to about 60^0 C and add oxalic acid solution dropwise to make the solution colour less. Cool and transfer to a 1 litre measuring flask and make volume to the mark. This solution contains 100ug Mn / ml (100 ppm). To prepare working standards, transfer 1,2,4 and 6 ml of the standard solution to a series of clean 100 ml volumetric flasks and dilute each to the mark with DTPA extracting solution.

Volume of stock Mn solution taken : 0 1 2 4 6ml

Concentration of Mn in solution : 0 1 2 4 6ug/ml (ppm)

Copper Standard Solution: Dissolve 0.392 copper sulphate ($CuSO_4 \cdot 5H_2O$) of AR grade in 400ml glass distilled water in a beaker. Transfer to a litre measuring flask and make volume to the mark with glass distilled water. This is a standard solution containing 100 ug Cu/ ml. To prepare working standards, transfer 1,2,4 and 6 ml of the standard solution to a series of clean 100 ml volumetric flasks and dilute each to the mark with DTPA extracting solution.

Volume of stock Cu solution taken : 0 1 2 4 6ml

Concentration of Cu in solution : 0 1 2 4 6ug/ml (ppm)

Extraction and Determination: Weigh 10 grams of air dried soil in a 125 ml conical flask or polypropylene bottle. Then add 20ml of the DTPA extracting solution. Cork the bottles or flask and place them upright on a horizontal shaker. Shake for two hours with a speed of 120 cycles per minute. Filter the suspension through Whatman no 42 filter paper. Keep the filtrate in polypropylene bottles to be analysed for Zn, Cu, Mn and Fe with an atomic absorption spectrophotometer. When samples need dilution before measurement, they should be diluted with DTPA solution to maintain a constant matrix.

4) PHYTOCHEMISTRY:

Preliminary phytochemical tests were carried out for the confirmation of starch, proteins, tannins, saponins, reducing sugars and anthroquinones on water extractives, while alkaloids, glycosides and flavonoids in alcoholic extractives. The results of these reactions were depicted in Table No. (22a & b).

i) Qualitative tests for Starch:

The plant material was finely ground and extracted with boiling methanol (methanol removes fats, fatty acids, salts, chlorophyll and inactive enzymes). After drying, the plant tissues were centrifuged with cold water and tested with iodine in 2% aqueous potassium iodide (Peach and Tracy, 1955).

ii) Qualitative tests for Protein: (Million's tests)

Millions reagent is a solution of mercuric nitrate in nitrate in nitric acid (it react specifically with any phenolic compound in which 3 and 5 positions are unsubstantiated). Proteins give red colouration with million's reagent.

Procedure: 2 ml of the test solution was boiled with the few drops of Million's reagent and colour was observed. (Trease and Evans, 1972).

iii) Qualitative tests for Tannins:

Plant part water extracts were treated with Ferric Chloride (Acidic) and observed for the presence of tannins (Trease and Evans, 1972).

iv) Qualitative tests for Saponins:

Water extracts of the plant material was vigorously shaken with few drops of neutral water. A permanent lather (foam) indicates the presence of saponins (Trease and Evans, 1972).

A portion of the residue obtained after evaporating the ethanol extracts was dissolved in water and shaken vigorously. A honeycomb, froth persisting for 15 min indicated the presence of saponins. A portion was dissolved in chloroform and filtered. A few drops of concentrated sulphuric acid and 1 ml. of acetic anhydride were added to 1 ml of iced filtrate. The appearance of blue or bluish green or reddish brown color showed the presence of saponins.

v) Qualitative tests for Flavonoids:

To 1 ml of ethanol extracts, few drops of concentrated HCL and Mg turning were added. The development of pink or magenta colour indicated the presence of flavonoids.

vi) Qualitative tests for Alkaloids:

Precipitation of alkaloids can be obtained with a variety of inorganic and organic reagents. Sometimes even from dilute solution. Among the inorganic precipitation reagents, to mention a few potassium mercuric iodide. (Mayer's reagent), and bismuth potassium iodide (Dragendorff's reagent) were used.

Characteristic colour reactions were obtained with the acid of dehydrating agents such as concentrated sulphuric acid, with oxidizing agent such as Nitric acid, with the combination of these two or other reagents, which will dehydrate and oxidize simultaneously and finally by treating with aldehyde or like compounds in the presence of dehydrating agents. The exact mechanism of precipitation reactions of alkaloids was not clearly understood. However, these reactions have proved to be an efficient tool in detection of alkaloids in plant tissues.

Reagents:

a. **Mayer's reagent:** 1.3g of $HgCl_2$ and 5 ml of KI were dissolved separately in 60 ml and 10 ml of distilled water respectively and both the solutions were mixed and diluted to 100ml.

b. **Dragendroff's reagent:** 8g of Bismuth nitrate was dissolved in 20 ml of concentrated HNO_3 and 27.2g of KI in 50 ml of distilled water. Both the solutions were allowed to stand till KIO_3 crystallized out. Supernatant was decanted and final volume was adjusted to 100 ml.

5) HIGH PERFORMANCE THIN LAYER CHROMATOGRAPHY (HPTLC):

An HPTLC technique was followed for the quantitative analysis and the confirmation of allelochemicals present in the studied plants (Passera, *et al.*, 1964).

HPTLC is a versatile separation technique included various steps as given below:

1) Plant extraction

2) Selection of HPTLC plates and sorbent

3) Sample preparation

4) Application of sample

5) Development (separation)

6) Detection including post-chromatographic derivatization

7) Quantitation

8) Documentation

1) Plant extraction:

The first step in the photochemical evaluation is extraction of the plant material. The choice of extraction method depends up on the nature of plant material and the compound (s) to be isolated.

2) Selection of HPTLC plates and sorbent:

Pre-coated plates with different support material (glass, aluminum, plastic) and with different sorbent layers are available in different format and thickness in various manufacturers. Usually plates with sorbent thickness of 100 – 250 µm are used for qualitative and quantitative analysis. However, for preparative TLC work, plates with sorbent thickness of 1.0 – 2.0 mm are available in addition to chemically modified layers. Aluminum sheet (0.1 mm thick) sheets as support offer the same advantage as polyester support but with increased temperature resistance. However, with eluents containing high concentration of mineral acids or concentrated ammonia. One may find problem, as they will chemically attack aluminum. Aluminum sheets are otherwise compatible with organic solvents and organic acids such as formic acid and acetic acid.

Plate size: Pre-coated TLC/ HPTLC plates in size of 20 × 20 cm with aluminum. It is always recommended to clear the plates before actual chromatography.

Activation of pre–coated plates: For the separation of compounds of herbal extracts pre-coated plates of silica gel G 60 are widely used especially the ones impregnated with phosphor (silica gel F $_{254}$, E. Merck). User UV at 254 nm, the resolved compounds whose absorption spectra overlap the excitation spectrum of phosphor are seen as dark bands against a yellow- green fluorescent background due to fluorescence quenching.

Freshly opened box of TLC/ HPTLC plates usually does not require activation. However, plates exposed to high humidity or kept on hand for long time may have to be activated by placing in oven at 110-120°C for 30 minutes prior to sample spotting (Sethi, 1996).

3) Sample Preparation:

Proper sample preparation is an important pre-requisite for success of thin layer chromatographic separation. The sample preparation procedure is to dissolve the dosage form with complete recovery of intact compound(s) of interest and minimum of matrix with a suitable concentration of analytic (s) for direct application on the HPTLC plate. Besides, maximizing the yield of analytic (s) in the selected solvent stability of analytics during extraction and analysis must be considered and ensured. Therefore, the choice of a suitable solvent for a given analysis is very important. For normal phase chromatography using silica gel pre-coated plates (more than 80-90% HPTLC analysis is done using silica gel as sorbent) solvent for dissolving the sample should be non-polar and volatile as far as possible. It is preferable to keep the solvent as simple as possible and quantity employed is limited to ensure complete extraction of analytics and minimum of extraneous component. Sample and reference substances should be dissolved in the same solvent to ensure comparable distribution at starting zones (Stahl, 1969).

4) Application of sample:

Sample application is the most critical step for obtaining good resolution for quantification by HPTLC. The sample should be completely transferred to the layer, however, under no circumstances, the application process should damage the layer, as damaged layer results in unevenly shaped spots. Wherever possible use of automatic application devices is recommended for quantitative analysis. While using graduated capillaries, one must ensure that they fill and empty completely. Usually application of 1–10 µl volume for TLC and 0.5–5 µl for HPTLC is recommended keeping the size of starting zone(s) down to minimum; 2–4 mm (TLC) and 0.5–1 mm (HPTLC) in the concentration range of 0.1–1 µg/µl for TLC/ HPTLC. However, volume and concentration primarily depend on the component under analysis and their sensitivity to various detection techniques.

5) Development (Mobile phase):

Poor grade of solvent used in preparing mobile phase have been found to decrease resolution, spot definition and R_f reproducibility. Mobile phase commonly called solvent system is traditionally selected by controlled process of trial and error and also based on one's own experience in the field. It is often possible that few layer-solvent combinations already reported in the literature for compounds of interest or similar compounds may be suitable in a given analytical problem with minor modifications. Nevertheless, it should not be forgotten that such conditions may have been chosen due to availability rather than suitability and often improvements are required. However, mobile phase should be chosen taking into consideration chemical properties of analytics and the sorbent layer. Use of mobile phase containing more than three or four components should normally be avoided, as it is often difficult to get reproducible rations of different components.

Pre-conditioning (Chamber saturation):

Chamber saturation has pronounced influence on the separation profile. When the plate is introduced into an unsaturated chamber, during the course of development, the solvent evaporates from the plate mainly at the solvent front. Therefore larger quantity of the solvent shall be required for a given distance hence, resulting is increase in R_f values. If the tank is saturated (by lining with filter paper) prior to development solvent vapors soon get uniformly distributed throughout the chamber. As soon as the plate is placed in such a saturated chamber, it soon gets pre-loaded with solvent vapors hence, less solvent shall be required to travel a particular distance resulting in lower R_f values. Time required for saturation will depend on the nature and composition of mobile phase and layer thickness (equilibration time increases with increase in layer thickness). Once the chromatogram is developed it should be handled with utmost care. Application of reagents if required has to be homogeneous ensuring uniform reaction and finally stabilizing of end reaction product. If heating of the plate after it is treated with the reagent is not uniform. There always exists risk of reaction in homogeneity on the plate. Usually drying cupboard or hot plates are employed. Hot plates with regulated range of temperature i.e. 50-190° C. 2° C are extensively being employed for heating the chromatogram.

6) Detection and visualization:

As soon as the development process is completed the plate is removed from the chamber contains the mobile phase of chloroform solvent and evaporated to remove the mobile phase completely. The zones can be located by various physical, chemical and biological i.e. physiological methods. There is apparently no difficulty in detecting colored substances or colorless substances in short wave ultra-violet (UV) region 254 nm and 366 nm or with intrinsic fluorescence such as riboflavin quinine sulphate.

7) Quantitation:

Spraying and dipping techniques are used for applying detection reagents. However, in addition to other reasons as enumerated below dipping followed by evaporation which is essential for both the precision and repeatability in ultimate quantitative analysis. Sample and standard are chromatographed on the same plate under similar conditions.

8) Documentation:

The use of application scheme and labeling every single chromatogram can avoid mistake in respect of order of application. It is preferable to apply each sample and reference solution twice by following data - pair method. A lead pencil can be used to write on the chromatoplate. The plate should never be marked below the starting point, as layer is likely to get damaged affecting chromatographic distribution of the substances under analysis which may ultimately lead to error in scanning. The best way to label the chromatoplate is to mark above the level of solvent point, immediately after development is completed, the solvent point should be marked both on left and right hand edges of the plate, this win facilitate calculation of R_f values. The practice of cutting a scratch across the whole layer is no longer in use. The type of plate, chamber system, composition of mobile phase, running time and detection method should all be recorded. HPTLC protocol format given in the text may be adopted for recording all the relevant data.

Following protocols were used for qualitative analysis of the chemicals.

1. Quantitative estimation of Steroids:

Sample preparation: Take 600mg of root, stem and leaf powder of each plant + 6ml Methanol, heat the solution at 70°C for 10 minutes, filter the solution and use the filtrate for sample application. 10µl of Sample was used for HPTLC.

Stationary Phase: Precoated Silica Gel TLC Plate (size 10x10 cm.)

Mobile Phase: Chloroform : Methanol : Water (v/v) 6.4 : 5 : 1

Developing Distance: 80 mm.

Tank saturation: 10 min.

Scanning wavelength: 254 nm, 366nm.

Derivatization Reagent: 5% Methanolic Sulphuric Acid reagent.

2. Quantitative estimation of Terpenoids:

Sample preparation: Take 600mg of root, stem and leaf powder of each plant + 6ml Methanol, heat the solution at 70°C for 10 minutes, filter the solution and use the filtrate for sample application. 10µl of Sample was used for HPTLC.

Stationary Phase: Precoated Silica Gel TLC Plate (size 10x10 cm.)

Mobile Phase: *n*-hexane : Ethyl Acetate (v/v) 10 : 10

Developing Distance: 80 mm.

Tank saturation: 10 min.

Scanning wavelength: 254 nm, 366nm.

Derivatization Reagent: 5% Methanolic Sulphuric Acid reagent.

3. Quantitative estimation of Lupeol from *Coccinia grandis*:

Sample preparation: Take 600mg of root, stem and leaf powder of *C.grandis* + 6ml Methanol, heat the solution at 70°C for 10 minutes, filter the solution and use the filtrate for sample application. 10µl of Sample was used for HPTLC.

Stationary Phase: Precoated Silica Gel TLC Plate (size 10x10 cm.)

Mobile Phase: Benzene : Ethyl Acetate (v/v) 19 : 1

Developing Distance: 80 mm.

Tank saturation: 10 min.

Scanning wavelength: 254 nm, 366nm.

Derivatization Reagent: 10% Methanolic Sulphuric Acid reagent.

Rf.: 3.09

Standard Lupeoul loaded: 10 µl.

For quantitative estimation of Steriods, Terpenoids and Lupeol win CATS Planar Chromatography was used. The detection was done on CAMAG TLC Scanner. The application position of sample was kept at 8.0 mm and solvent front position at 80.0 mm. The CAMAG TLC Scanner 3 "Scanner3_070408 (1.14.26) instrument was executed by Anchrom. On this, number of tracks were followed, position of first track X at 18.7 mm, distance between tracks 13.3 mm, scan start position Y at 5.0 mm, scan end position Y at 85.0 m, slit dimension at 6.00 ×0.30 mm, Micro Optimize optical system used light, Scanning speed kept at 20 mm/s and data resolution at 100 µm/step.

For the measurement of values of each sample of wavelength 580nm, lamp W, measurement type remission, measurement mode Absorption, Optical filter second order, detector mode automatic Pm high voltage of 318V.

6) STATISTICAL ANALYSIS:

Analysis of variance (ANOVA) is a useful and most versatile method of statistical inference. It is useful for analyzing observational data of several types. There are different techniques for testing the difference among means in an ANOVA (called multiple comparisons).

In the present investigation statistical tests were applied to find out the mean values of radicle and hypocotyl of test plants under the influence of treatments of different bioassay. Data were analyzed by one-way ANOVA; Duncan Multiple Range Test (DMRT) by using SPSS software. Data of Radicle and Hypocotyl were expressed by Mean ± Standard Error (n = 3). Values followed by the same letter (a, b, c, d and e) were not significantly different at 5% level.

CHAPTER FOUR

Results

To know the allelopathic potentiality of four major noxious medicinally important plants of family Cucurbitaceae are studied in the present investigation.

A. *Citrullus colocynthis*

B. *Coccinia grandis*

C. *Cucumis trigonus*

D. *Diplocyclos palmatus*

Usually all these selected plants are fields climber, and are found to be growing in cultivated as well as in the fallow lands. They do not only affect the growth and development of agricultural crops but also affects the crop yields.

It is observed and confirmed that these plants clearly demonstrates an inhibitory effect (allelopathic effects) on root and shoot of test crop. In addition, seed germination and seedling growth of test crop *Phaseolus aconitifolius* Jacq. variety – 'Abhaya'. is also affected.

To evaluate the allelopathic activity of these plants, following five types of bioassays were carried out in the laboratory.

1. Phytoextracts Bioassay.

2. Leachates Bioassay.

3. Decomposition Bioassay.

4. Volatilization Bioassay.

5. Root exudation Bioassay (Root zone soil).

The allelopathic pattern varied in each plant species in view of the inhibitor content differing in the phytoextracts, leachates, root exudates, decaying plant parts and volatilization. In all cases, the seed germination and seedling growth of *Phaseolus aconitifolius* was seriously hampered. These inhibitory effects may be coinciding with their dominance in each ecosystem.

A. *Citrullus colocynthis*

1) Phytoextracts Bioassay: During phytoextracts bioassay studies it was found that major toxicity is observed in 1:2.5% of phytoextracts of all three parts i.e. root, stem and leaves. However, the order of inhibition is root > leaf > stem. The results indicated that all extracts significantly inhibits seed germination and seedling growth of *Phaseolus aconitifolius* and exhibits according to increase in concentrations. It is also observed that the major toxicity is caused at 2.0% and 2.5% w/v of phytoextracts of all three parts. The root extracts shows greater inhibitory on seed germination and seedling growth of *Phaseolus*. At the lower concentrations of inhibitor solutions significant effects was not observed during seed germination and seedling growth of test crop while at the higher concentrations root extracts are more toxic than stem and leaf extracts. However, the order of inhibition of phytoextracts of *Citrullus* is root > leaf > stem. (Table No. 1a, b and c) (Plate No. VI, VII and VIII)

PLATE VI

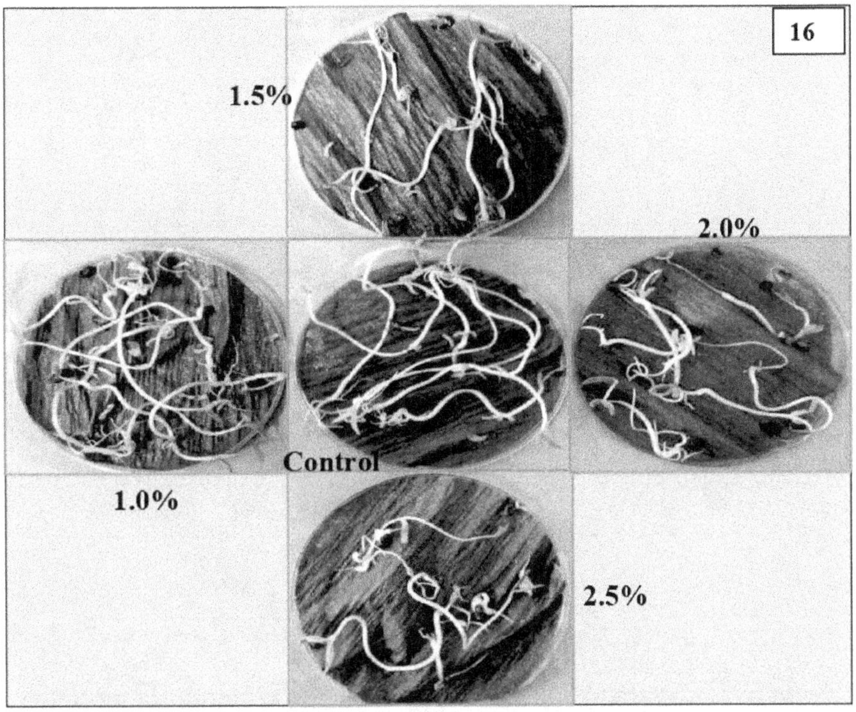

Fig. No.16: Root Phytoextracts bioassay of *Citrullus colocynthis*

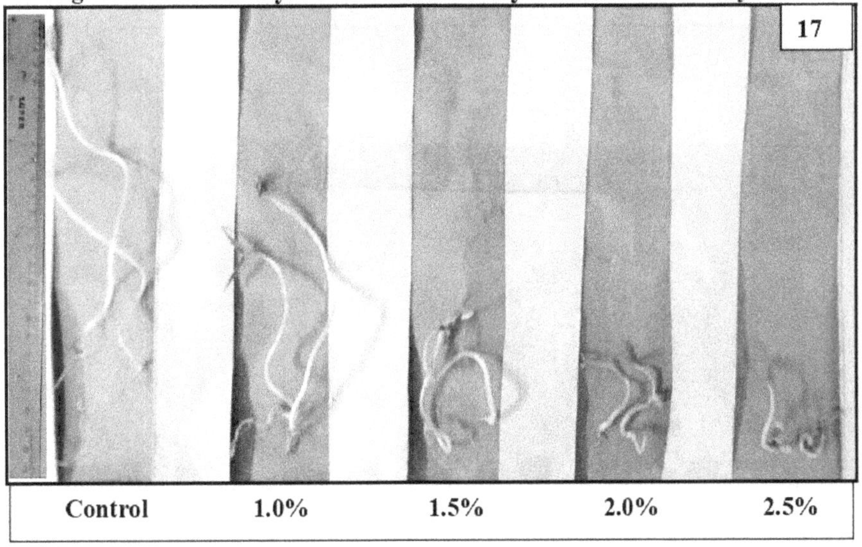

Fig. No.17: Showing relative length of *Phaseolus aconitifolius* seedling

PLATE VII

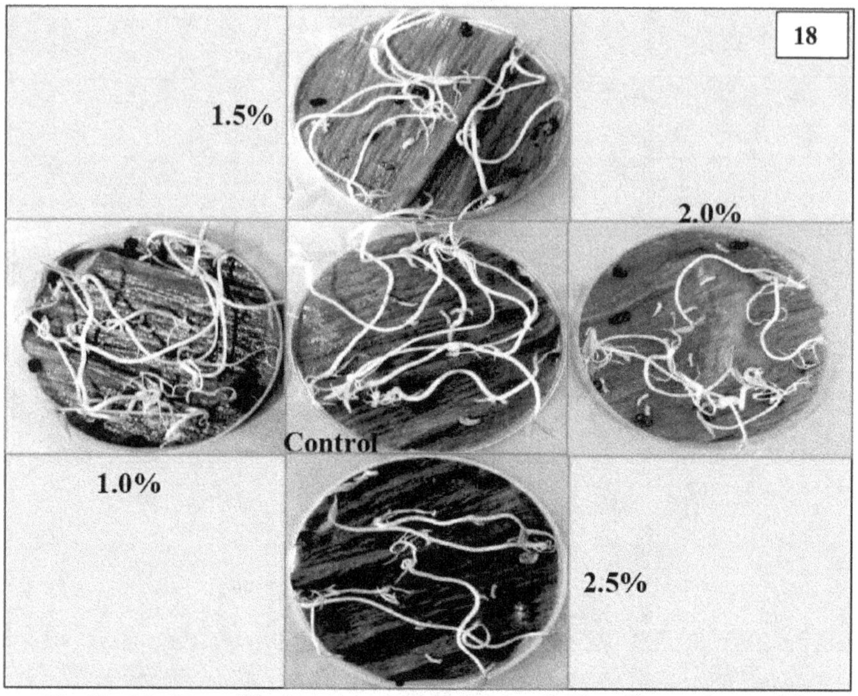

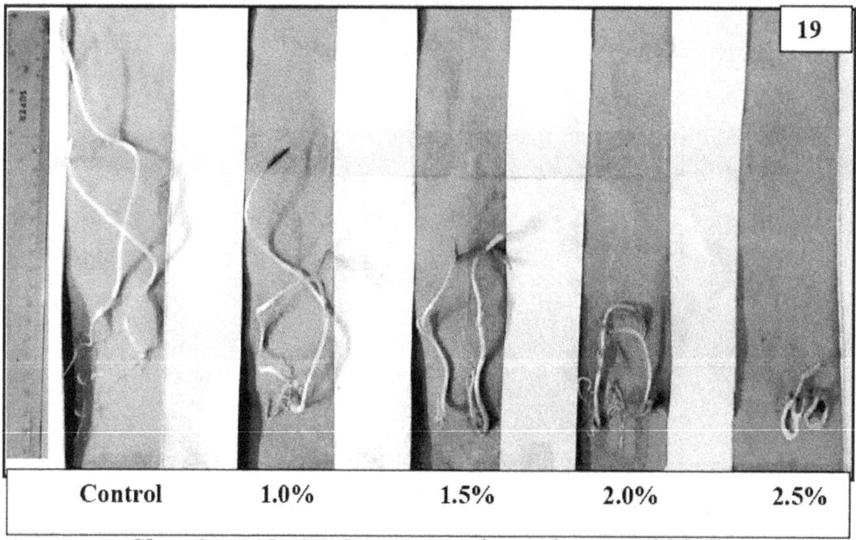

Fig. No.18: Stem Phytoextracts bioassay of *Citrullus colocynthis*

Fig. No.19: Showing relative length of *Phaseolus aconitifolius* seedling

PLATE VIII

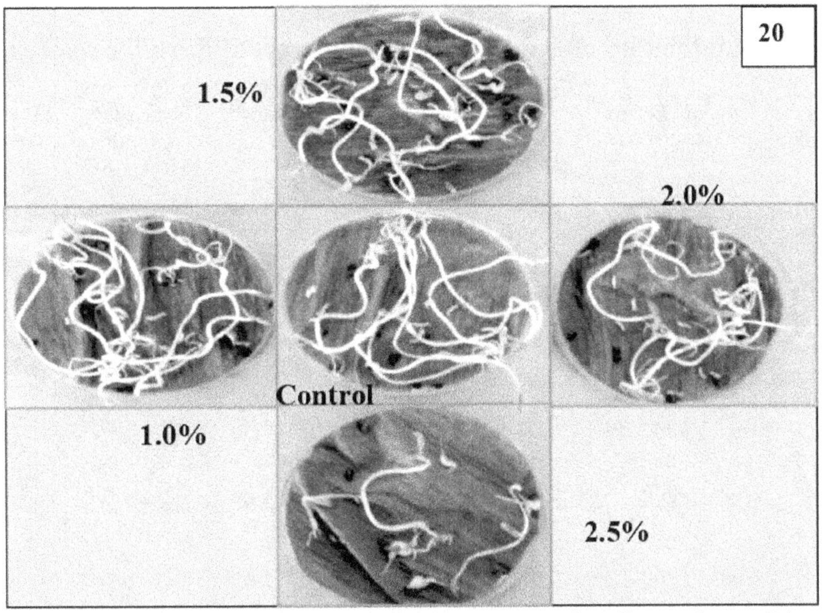

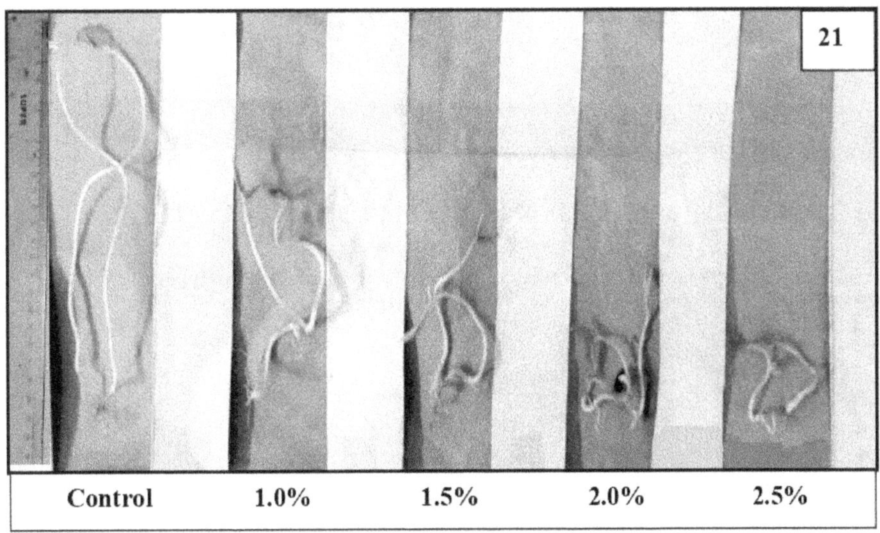

Fig. No. 20:Leaf Phytoextracts bioassay of *Citrullus colocynthis*

Fig. No. 21: Showing relative length of *Phaseolus aconitifolius* seedling

Phytoextract Bioassay

Table No.1a: Inhibitory effects of Root Phytoextract of *Citrullus colocynthis* on *Phaseolus aconitifolius* seeds.

Extract Concentration (%)	Radicle Length Mean (cm)			Radicle Length (Mean ± SE)	Hypocotyls Length Mean (cm)			Hypocotyls Length (Mean ± SE)	Average Seed Germination (%)
	I	II	III		I	II	III		
Control	5.29	4.93	5.23	5.1 ± 0.1^a	8.16	7.44	8.25	7.9 ± 0.2^a	93.33
1.0%	2.65	3.27	3.96	3.2 ± 0.3^b	4.96	4.18	5.06	4.7 ± 0.2^b	93.33
1.5%	2.23	3.03	3.11	2.7 ± 0.2^{bc}	4.71	4.99	4.97	4.8 ± 0.09^b	93.33
2.0%	2.97	1.90	2.70	2.5 ± 0.3^{bc}	4.83	3.09	3.80	3.9 ± 0.5^b	83.33
2.5%	3.01	1.56	1.60	2.0 ± 0.4^c	4.93	2.92	2.66	3.5 ± 0.7^b	76.66

Data were analyzed by one-way ANOVA; Duncan Multiple Range Test (DMRT) using SPSS software. Data of Radicle and Hypocotyls were expressed by Mean±SE ($n = 3$). Values followed by the same letter were not significantly different at 5% level (DMRT).

Table No.1b: Inhibitory effects of Stem Phytoextract of *Citrullus colocynthis* on *Phaseolus aconitifolius* seeds.

Extract Concentration (%)	Radicle Length Mean (cm)			Radicle Length (Mean ± SE)	Hypocotyls Length Mean (cm)			Hypocotyls Length (Mean ± SE)	Average Seed Germination (%)
	I	II	III		I	II	III		
Control	4.87	5.07	5.36	5.1 ± 0.1^a	5.69	6.86	7.06	6.5 ± 0.4^a	100
1.0%	3.24	3.41	3.48	3.3 ± 0.07^b	5.22	5.34	5.83	5.4 ± 0.1^{ab}	93.33
1.5%	3.01	3.33	3.10	3.1 ± 0.09^b	5.02	4.70	4.77	4.8 ± 0.09^{bc}	86.66
2.0%	3.22	2.59	1.95	2.5 ± 0.3^b	4.99	3.38	3.27	3.8 ± 0.5^c	86.66
2.5%	3.56	2.54	1.74	2.6 ± 0.5^b	4.77	3.01	2.15	3.3 ± 0.7^c	80.00

Data were analyzed by one-way ANOVA; Duncan Multiple Range Test (DMRT) using SPSS software. Data of Radicle and Hypocotyls were expressed by Mean±SE ($n = 3$). Values followed by the same letter were not significantly different at 5% level (DMRT).

Table No.1c: Inhibitory effects of Leaf Phytoextract of *Citrullus colocynthis* on *Phaseolus aconitifolius* seeds.

Extract Concentration (%)	Radicle Length Mean (cm)			Radicle Length (Mean ± SE)	Hypocotyls Length Mean (cm)			Hypocotyls Length (Mean ± SE)	Average Seed Germination (%)
	I	II	III		I	II	III		
Control	4.98	5.96	6.70	5.8 ± 0.4[a]	5.85	7.36	8.38	7.1 ± 0.7[a]	100
1.0%	3.31	3.40	4.22	3.6 ± 0.2[b]	7.55	6.77	7.32	7.2 ± 0.2[a]	100
1.5%	3.69	3.60	4.44	3.9 ± 0.2[b]	7.18	6.65	6.26	6.6 ± 0.2[ab]	100
2.0%	2.81	2.30	1.96	2.3 ± 0.2[c]	6.40	5.26	4.70	5.4 ± 0.5[b]	76.66
2.5%	1.59	1.25	1.09	1.3 ± 0.1[d]	4.20	3.85	3.02	3.6 ± 0.3[c]	73.33

Data were analyzed by one-way ANOVA; Duncan Multiple Range Test (DMRT) using SPSS software. Data of Radicle and Hypocotyls were expressed by Mean±SE (n = 3). Values followed by the same letter were not significantly different at 5% level (DMRT).

2) Leachates Bioassay: It is observed that leaf leachates fully suppress the seed germination as well overall seedling growth of *Phaseolus*. The leachates of root, stem and leaves significantly affect the seed germination and seedling growth of *Phaseolus*. It is observed that the leaf leachate fully hampered the radicle growth and also suppresses the seed germination. The root and stem leachates also effectively inhibited the seedling growth. The magnitude of inhibition from leachates followed the order: leaf > root > stem. The reduction in germination might be due to water – soluble allelochemicals in leachates. However, among all three types of leachates leaf leachates did not allow seed germination and seedling growth of *Phaseolus*. (Table No.5) (Plate No. XVIII)

PLATE XVIII

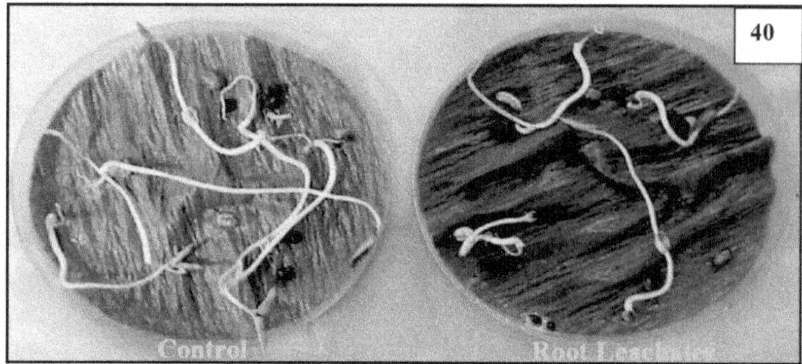

Fig. No.40: *Citrullus colocynthis* root Leachates bioassay on *Phaseolus aconitifolius* seeds.

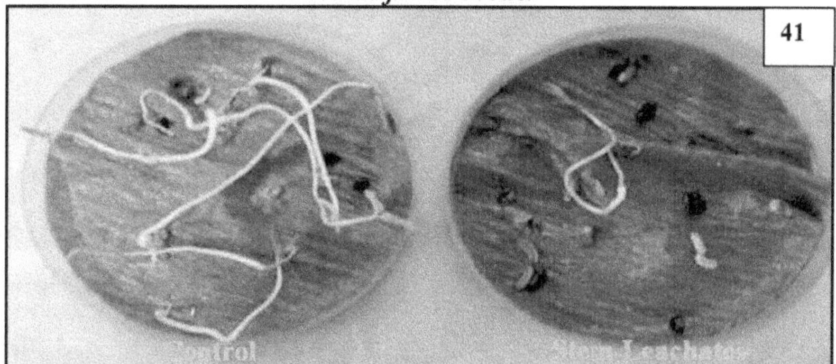

Fig. No.41: *Citrullus colocynthis* Stem Leachates bioassay on *Phaseolus aconitifolius* seeds.

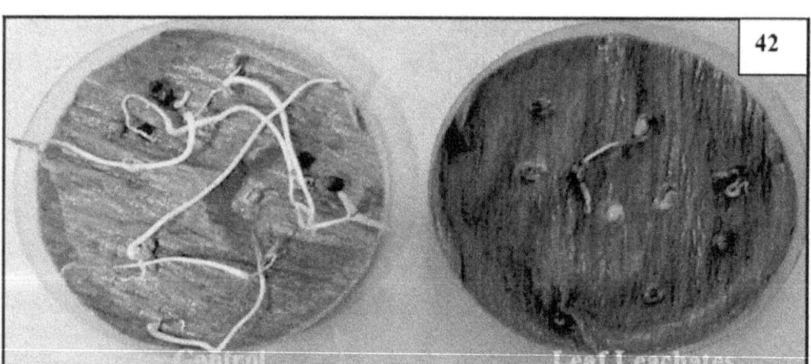

Fig. No.42: *Citrullus colocynthis* Leaf Leachates bioassay on *Phaseolus aconitifolius* seeds.

Leachates Bioassay

Table No. 5: Inhibitory effects of Leachates of *Citrullus colocynthis* on *Phaseolus aconitifolius* seeds.

Types of Leachates	Radicle Length Mean (cm)			Radicle Length (Mean ± SE)	Hypocotyls Length Mean (cm)			Hypocotyls Length (Mean ± SE)	Average Seed Germination (%)
	I	II	III		I	II	III		
Control	5.13	3.64	5.39	4.7 ± 0.5^a	8.60	6.77	7.77	7.7 ± 0.5^a	100
Root	1.31	0.84	1.06	1.0 ± 0.1^b	3.21	2.07	1.95	2.4 ± 0.4^b	73.33
Stem	1.33	1.09	1.19	1.2 ± 0.06^b	2.68	2.31	2.74	2.5 ± 0.1^b	66.66
Leaf	0.26	0.61	0.36	0.4 ± 0.1^b	1.84	1.81	1.85	1.8 ± 0.01^b	63.33

Data were analyzed by one-way ANOVA; Duncan Multiple Range Test (DMRT) using SPSS software. Data of Radicle and Hypocotyls were expressed by Mean±SE ($n = 3$). Values followed by the same letter were not significantly different at 5% level (DMRT).

3) Decomposition (Decaying plant parts): It has been observed that overall seedling growth as well as seed germination showed appreciable inhibitory effects at higher amount of dry material of plant parts of *Citrullus colocynthis*. The germination percentage as well as seedling growth is significantly reduces in higher amount of plant material allowed for decomposing. The remarkable inhibition in seedling growth is found at 16g and 32g plant material. Incorporation of the plant material in the soil significantly reduces more radicle length than hypocotyl elongation. The effect is more pronounced at higher rates (32g plant material/ 250g of soil) on seedling growth. However, at low rate of plant material (2g and 4g/ 250g of soil) slightly affected seed germination percentage while increased or not significantly inhibited seedling growth of *Phaseolus*. (Table No.9) (Plate No. XXII: Figs.52)

PLATE XXII

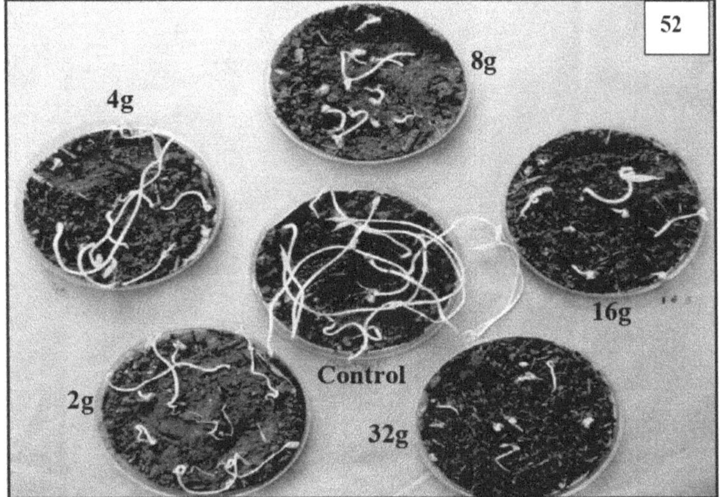

Fig. No.52: Decomposition bioassay: *Phaseolus* **seeds showing relative length in different quantities of compost of** *Citrullus colocynthis*.

Decomposition Bioassay

Table No. 9: Inhibitory effects of Decomposition of *Citrullus colocynthis* on *Phaseolus aconitifolius* seeds.

Quantity of plant parts in decomposition (g/250g soil)	Radicle Length Mean (cm)			Radicle Length (Mean ± SE)	Hypocotyls Length Mean (cm)			Hypocotyls Length (Mean ± SE)	Average Seed Germination (%)
	I	II	III		I	II	III		
Control	8.72	8.86	9.08	8.8 ± 0.1[a]	11.21	11.48	11.55	11.4 ± 0.1[a]	100
2g	6.38	6.90	6.67	6.6 ± 0.1[b]	9.10	9.94	10.28	9.7 ± 0.3[b]	96.66
4g	5.50	5.61	5.91	5.6 ± 0.1[c]	7.11	6.99	8.05	7.3 ± 0.3[c]	93.33
8g	3.33	3.15	3.57	3.3 ± 0.2[d]	4.41	4.19	5.25	4.6 ± 0.3[d]	83.33
16g	1.91	2.15	2.25	2.1 ± 0.1[e]	3.18	3.76	3.85	3.5 ± 0.2[e]	66.66
32g	0.63	1.08	1.07	0.9 ± 0.1[f]	1.62	2.64	2.49	2.2 ± 0.3[f]	43.33

Data were analyzed by one-way ANOVA: Duncan Multiple Range Test (DMRT) using SPSS software. Data of Radicle and Hypocotyls were expressed by Mean±SE ($n = 3$). Values followed by the same letter were not significantly different at 5% level (DMRT).

4) Volatilization: The results of volatilization bioassay indicated that water kept with plant material in airtight jar affects the germination and seedling growth significantly than soil, which indicates that water absorbs the volatile substances more. Water kept with plant material of *Citrullus colocynthis* in airtight jar affects seed germination and seedling growth significantly than soil. This indicates that water absorbs some volatile substance(s)morefrom the plant. Remarkable inhibitory effects on seed germination and seedling growth were noted. A considerable reduction in radicle growth was found in *Citrullus*. (Table No.13) (Plate No. XXIV)

PLATE XXIV

Fig. No. 56: Volatilization bioassay

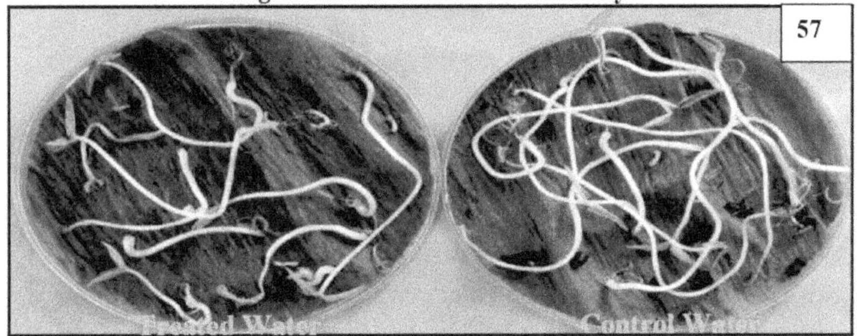

Fig. No. 57: Water Volatilization bioassay of *Citrullus colocynthis* on *Phaseolus aconitifolius* seeds.

Fig. No. 58: Soil Volatilization bioassay of *Citrullus colocynthis* on *Phaseolus aconitifolius* seeds.

Volatilization Bioassay

Table No. 13: Inhibitory effects of Volatilization of *Citrullus colocynthis* on *Phaseolus aconitifolius* seeds.

Types of bioassay	Radicle Length Mean (cm)			Radicle Length (Mean ± SE)	Hypocotyls Length Mean (cm)			Hypocotyls Length (Mean ± SE)	Average Seed Germination (%)
	I	II	III		I	II	III		
Control water	4.08	4.33	3.40	3.9 ± 0.2^a	6.48	6.58	5.55	6.2 ± 0.3^a	100
Treated water	1.99	2.07	2.84	2.3 ± 0.2^b	3.66	3.77	5.10	4.1 ± 0.4^b	83.33
Control soil	4.53	4.77	5.47	4.9 ± 0.2^a	7.33	7.58	8.29	7.7 ± 0.2^a	100
Treated soil	2.09	2.44	2.59	2.3 ± 0.1^b	4.32	4.15	4.85	4.4 ± 0.2^b	93.33

Data were analyzed by one-way ANOVA; Duncan Multiple Range Test (DMRT) using SPSS software. Data of Radicle and Hypocotyls were expressed by Mean±SE ($n = 3$). Values followed by the same letter were not significantly different at 5% level (DMRT).

5) Root zone soil (Root exudation) Bioassay: Seeds kept in root zone soil showed considerable inhibition of seed germination and seedling growth of test crop. It was also found that the radicle length was more affected than hypocotyls. Root exudates of *Citrullus colocynthis* significantly inhibited seed germination and seedling growth of test crop. The root exudates significantly affect the radicle and hypocotyls length over control. The major phytotoxicity was observed in radicle length than hypocotyls elongation. (Table No. 17) (Plate No. XXVIII: Figs. 65.)

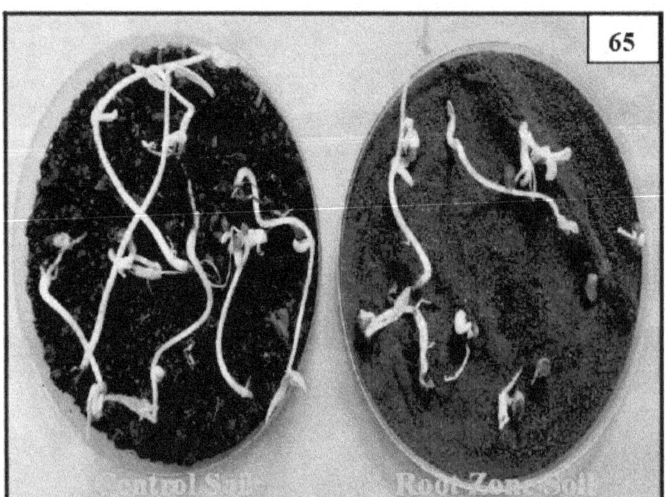

Fig. No. 65: *Citrullus colocynthis* Root Zone Soil on *Phaseolus* seeds

Plate No. XXVIII

Root Exudation Bioassay (Root Zone Soil)

Table No. 17: Inhibitory effects of Root Exudation of *Citrullus colocynthis* on *Phaseolus aconitifolius* seeds.								
Concentration (%)	Radicle Length Mean (cm)			Radicle Length (Mean $\pm$ SE)	Hypocotyls Length Mean (cm)			Hypocotyls Length (Mean $\pm$ SE)	Average Seed Germination (%)
	I	II	III		I	II	III		
Control soil	5.89	4.77	5.21	5.2 $\pm$ 0.3	8.82	7.07	7.34	7.7 $\pm$ 0.5	100
Root exudation (Root zone soil)	2.37	2.75	2.06	2.3 $\pm$ 0.1	4.81	4.27	4.43	4.5 $\pm$ 0.1	90.00

6) Root zone soil analysis: There is significant difference in pH of soil were (6.13) shows acidic in nature. The value of EC (0.58) was much reduced in case of *Citrullus colocynthis*. There was some remarkable difference in the value of Organic Carbon contents (0.60) over control soil (0.61-0.80). Phosphorous contents (11 Kg/ac) in the root zone soils also showed appreciable reduction over control soil (51-65 Kg/ac). The amount of Potassium (154 Kg/ac) contents in the root zone soils also showed significant reduction over control soil (240-300). Zinc (1.86 ppm), Copper (3.97 ppm), Iron (11.18 ppm) and Manganese (22.85 ppm) content in the root zone soil of *Citrullus colocynthis* showed significant reduction as compare to control soil. (Table No. 21)

7) Phytochemical Studies: The root phytoextracts and leaf leachates of *Citrullus colocynthis* had greater inhibitory effects on seed germination as well as seedling growth of *Phaseolus*. The inhibitory effect might be due to the excessive presence of starch, tannins, saponins, flavanoids and alkaloids which acts as allelochemicals. Besides, allelochemicals in aqueous root extract and leaf leachates might inhibit some physiological process responsible for seed germination. (Table No. 22a)

B). *Coccinia grandis*

1) Phytoextracts Bioassay: The root, stem and leaf phytoextract bioassay indicats that, major inhibitory activity was caused by 1:2.5% of phytoextract of each part. However, the order of inhibition is root > stem > leaf. The effects of phytoextracts of all three parts of *Coccinia grandis* show greater inhibitory effects on seed germination and seedling growth of *Phaseolus aconitifolius* and exhibits according to increase in concentrations. It is also observed that the major toxicity is caused at 2.0% and 2.5% w/v of phytoextracts of all three parts. The root extracts shows greater inhibitory on seed germination and seedling growth of *Phaseolus*. Root extract markedly inhibited the radicle length at various concentration than hypocotyls growth of *Phaseolus*. At the lower concentrations of inhibitor solutions significant effects was not observed during seed germination and seedling growth of test crop while at the higher concentrations root extracts are more toxic than stem and leaf extracts. However, the order of inhibition of phytoextracts of *Coccinia* is root > stem > leaf. (Table No. 2a, b and c) (Plate No. IX, X and XI)

PLATE IX

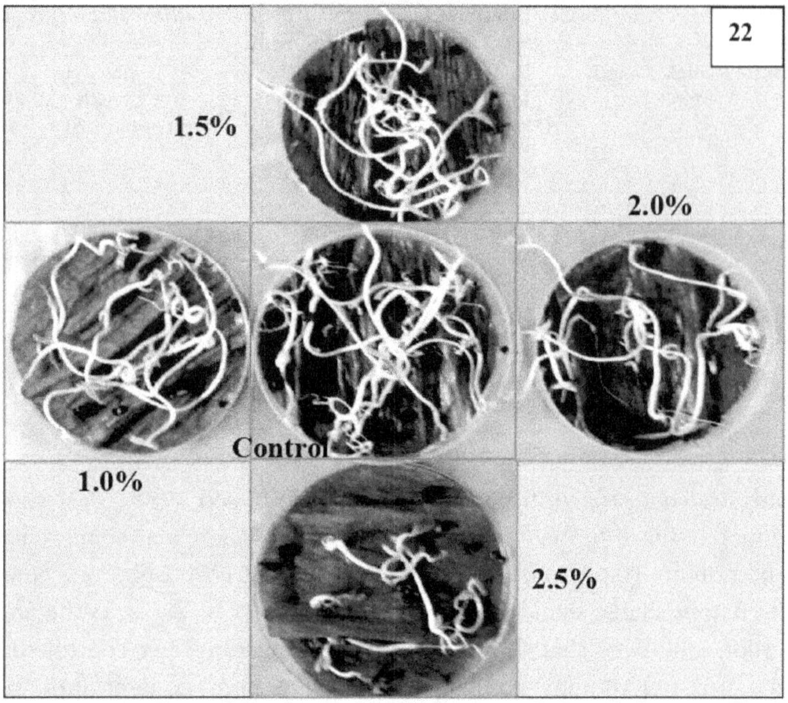

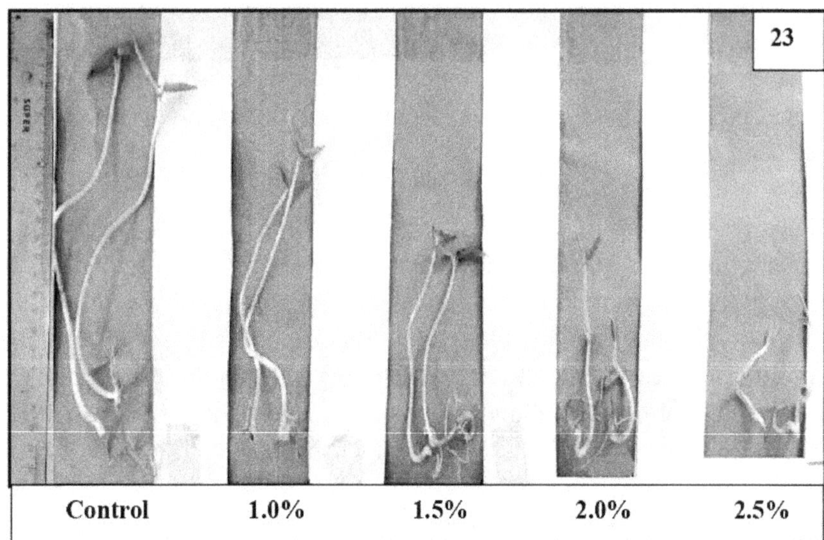

Fig. No.22: **Root Phytoextracts bioassay of** *Coccinia grandis*

Fig. No.23: **Showing relative length of** *Phaseolus aconitifolius* **seedling**

PLATE X

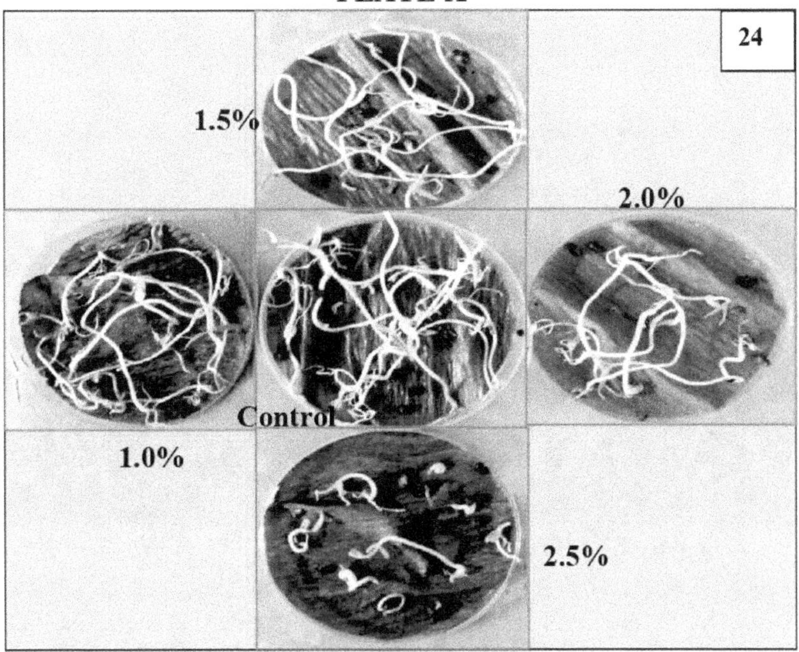

Fig. No.24:Stem Phytoextracts bioassay of *Coccinia grandis*

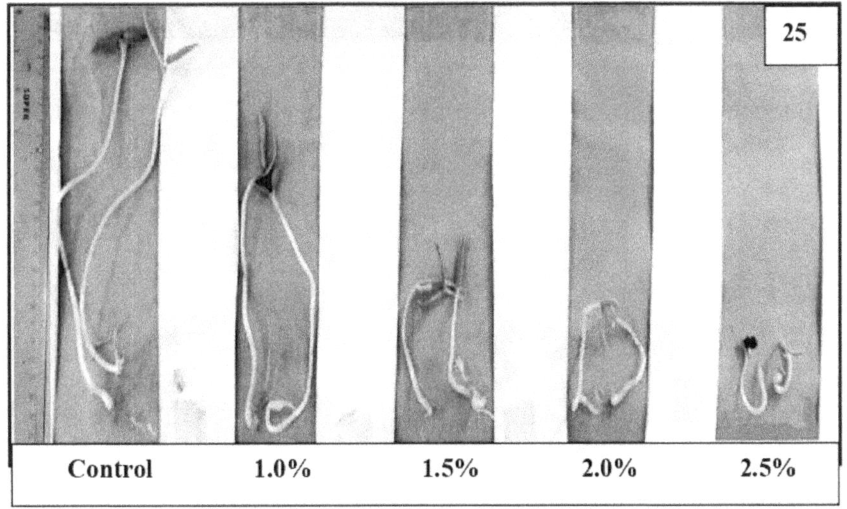

Fig. No.25: Showing relative length of *Phaseolus aconitifolius* seedling

PLATE XI

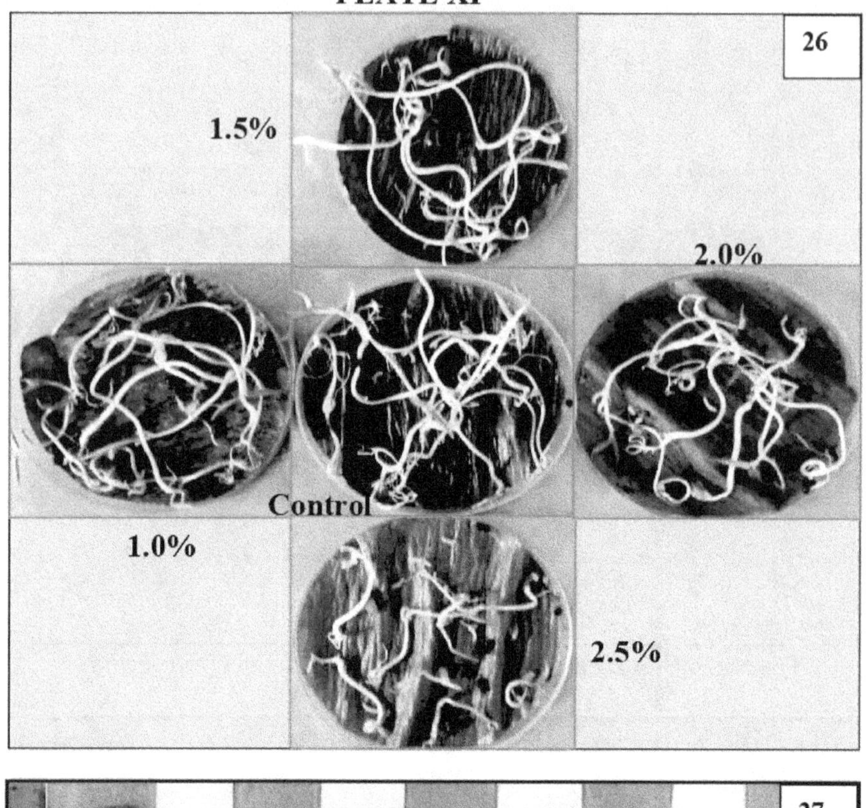

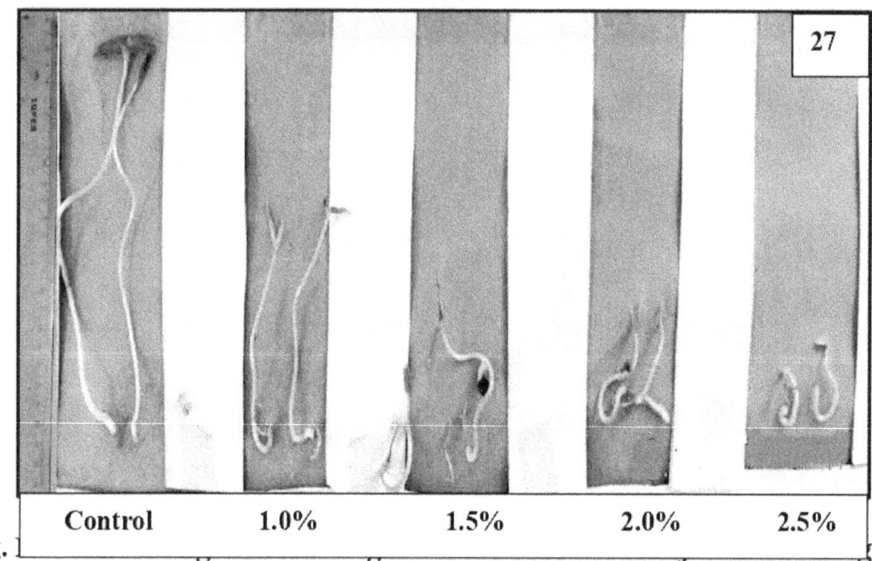

Table No.2a: Inhibitory effects of Root Phytoextract of *Coccinia grandis* on *Phaseolus aconitifolius* seeds.

Extract Concentration (%)	Radicle Length Mean (cm)			Radicle Length (Mean ± SE)	Hypocotyls Length Mean (cm)			Hypocotyls Length (Mean ± SE)	Average Seed Germination (%)
	I	II	III		I	II	III		
Control	5.12	4.84	4.46	4.8 ± 0.2^a	5.12	5.57	6.05	5.5 ± 0.2^a	100
1.0%	3.58	3.21	3.16	3.3 ± 0.1^b	4.89	4.27	4.61	4.5 ± 0.1^a	96.66
1.5%	3.13	2.94	3.44	3.1 ± 0.1^b	5.61	5.07	5.73	5.4 ± 0.2^b	96.66
2.0%	2.45	2.04	2.42	2.3 ± 0.1^c	3.63	3.77	3.24	3.5 ± 0.1^c	76.66
2.5%	2.56	1.62	1.45	1.9 ± 0.3^c	3.76	2.83	2.37	2.9 ± 0.4^c	73.33

Data were analyzed by one-way ANOVA; Duncan Multiple Range Test (DMRT) using SPSS software. Data of Radicle and Hypocotyls were expressed by Mean±SE (n = 3). Values followed by the same letter were not significantly different at 5% level (DMRT).

Table No.2b: Inhibitory effects of Stem Phytoextract of *Coccinia grandis* on *Phaseolus aconitifolius* seeds.

Extract Concentration (%)	Radicle Length Mean (cm)			Radicle Length (Mean ± SE)	Hypocotyls Length Mean (cm)			Hypocotyls Length (Mean ± SE)	Average Seed Germination (%)
	I	II	III		I	II	III		
Control	3.90	4.97	5.18	4.7 ± 0.3^a	5.81	6.44	6.79	6.3 ± 0.2^a	100
1.0%	3.98	3.32	3.72	3.6 ± 0.1^b	5.31	6.18	6.45	5.9 ± 0.3^a	96.66
1.5%	3.04	3.24	3.13	3.1 ± 0.05^{bc}	3.8	5.51	3.24	4.1 ± 0.6^b	86.66
2.0%	3.18	2.78	2.37	2.7 ± 0.2^c	4.31	3.69	3.47	3.8 ± 0.2^b	83.33
2.5%	3.11	2.58	1.97	2.5 ± 0.3^c	5.21	3.5	2.96	3.8 ± 0.6^b	80.00

Data were analyzed by one-way ANOVA; Duncan Multiple Range Test (DMRT) using SPSS software. Data of Radicle and Hypocotyls were expressed by Mean±SE (n = 3). Values followed by the same letter were not significantly different at 5% level (DMRT).

Table No.2c: Inhibitory effects of Leaf Phytoextract of *Coccinia grandis* on *Phaseolus aconitifolius* seeds.

Extract Concentration (%)	Radicle Length Mean (cm)			Radicle Length (Mean $\pm$ SE)	Hypocotyls Length Mean (cm)			Hypocotyls Length (Mean $\pm$ SE)	Average Seed Germination (%)
	I	II	III		I	II	III		
Control	5.10	4.89	5.90	5.2 ± 0.3^a	6.50	6.80	7.80	7.0 ± 0.3^a	100
1.0%	2.83	3.06	4.25	3.3 ± 0.4^b	5.24	2.04	5.43	4.2 ± 1.0^b	90.00
1.5%	2.30	2.34	4.03	2.8 ± 0.5^{bc}	4.89	4.06	4.65	4.5 ± 0.2^b	86.66
2.0%	3.43	2.39	2.22	2.6 ± 0.3^{bc}	4.12	4.23	4.12	4.6 ± 0.03^b	86.66
2.5%	1.56	2.29	2.21	2.0 ± 0.2^c	4.03	3.45	4.01	3.8 ± 0.1^b	83.33

Data were analyzed by one-way ANOVA: Duncan Multiple Range Test (DMRT) using SPSS software. Data of Radicle and Hypocotyls were expressed by Mean±SE (n = 3). Values followed by the same letter were not significantly different at 5% level (DMRT).

2) Leachates Bioassay: The leachates of root, stem and leaves significantly affects the seed germination and seedling growth of test crop. It is observed that root leachates fully suppress the seed germination as well overall seedling growth of *Phaseolus*. Root leachates are inhibitorier than stem and leaf leachates. The leachates of root, stem and leaves significantly affects the seed germination and seedling growth of *Phaseolus*. Highest inhibition is found in root leachates followed by stem and leaf leachates. It is observed that the root leachate fully hampered the radicle growth and also suppresses the seed germination. The seedling growth was progressively decreased than seed germination in all three types of leachates. The radicle lengths are more affected than hypocotyls elongation. However, the magnitude of inhibition from leachates followed the order: root > stem > leaf. The reduction in germination might be due to water – soluble allelochemicals in leachates. (Table No.6) (Plate No. XIX)

PLATE XIX

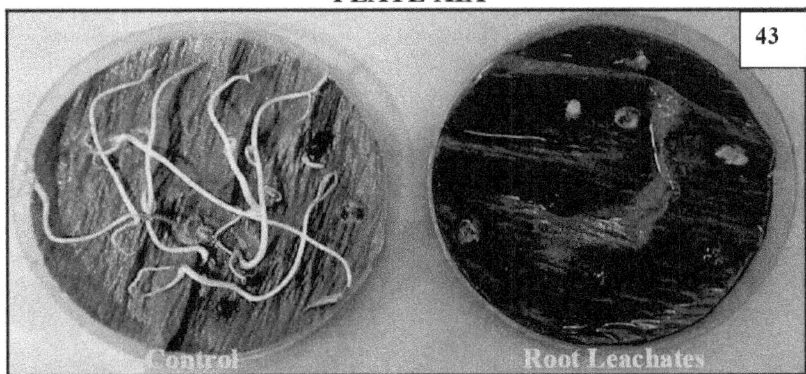

Fig. No.43: *Coccinia grandis* root Leachates bioassay on *Phaseolus aconitifolius* seeds.

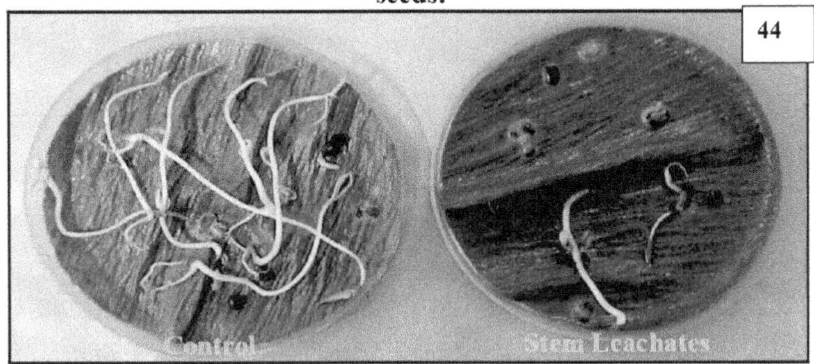

Fig. No.44: *Coccinia grandis* Stem Leachates bioassay on *Phaseolus aconitifolius* seeds.

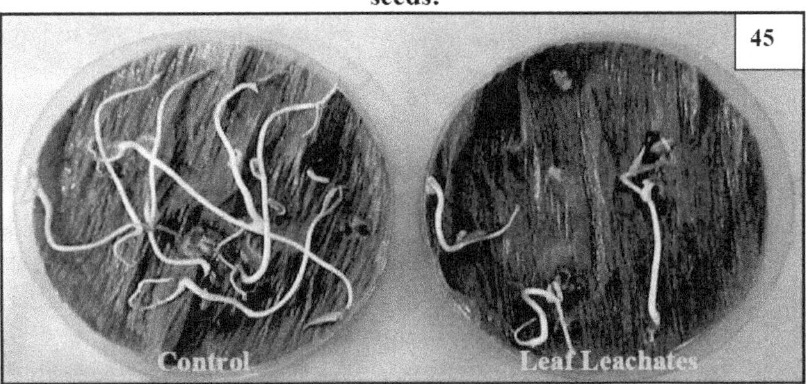

Fig. No.45: *Coccinia grandis* Leaf Leachates bioassay on *Phaseolus aconitifolius* seeds.

Table No. 6: Inhibitory effects of Leachates of *Coccinia grandis* on *Phaseolus aconitifolius* seeds.

Types of Leachates	Radicle Length Mean (cm)			Radicle Length (Mean ± SE)	Hypocotyls Length Mean (cm)			Hypocotyls Length (Mean ± SE)	Average Seed Germination (%)
	I	II	III		I	II	III		
Control	4.71	4.89	5.18	4.9 ± 0.1^a	6.86	7.10	7.57	7.1 ± 0.2^a	100
Root	0.48	0.36	0.28	0.3 ± 0.05^d	2.17	2.07	1.92	2.0 ± 0.07^d	46.66
Stem	1.03	1.34	1.07	1.1 ± 0.09^c	3.25	3.30	2.92	3.1 ± 0.1^c	70.00
Leaf	1.67	1.62	1.44	1.5 ± 0.06^b	4.33	3.90	3.45	3.8 ± 0.2^b	80.00

Data were analyzed by one-way ANOVA: Duncan Multiple Range Test (DMRT) using SPSS software. Data of Radicle and Hypocotyls were expressed by Mean±SE (n = 3). Values followed by the same letter were not significantly different at 5% level (DMRT).

3) Decomposition (Decaying plant parts): The results of decaying plant parts of *Coccinia grandis* shows that there is appreciable reduction in seed germination and seedling length was highly suppressed due to 16g and 32g plant part mixed in 250g of soil. The decaying plant parts added in the soil shows more pronounced inhibitory effects on seed germination than seedling growth of *Phaseolus*. The maximum inhibitions in germination were affected in 16g and 32g of plant material incorporated in the soil. Decayed plant materials at low rates 2g and 4g had no much harmful effect on seed germination as well as seedling growth of test crop. Greater inhibitory effect was found on radicle length with increased amount of plant parts in the soil. Perhaps, it may be due to large quantities of harmful chemicals were accumulated in the soil. However, the maximum inhibition in seed germination and seedling growth was found at 32g plant materials added in the soil. (Table No.10) (Plate No. XXII: Figs 53.)

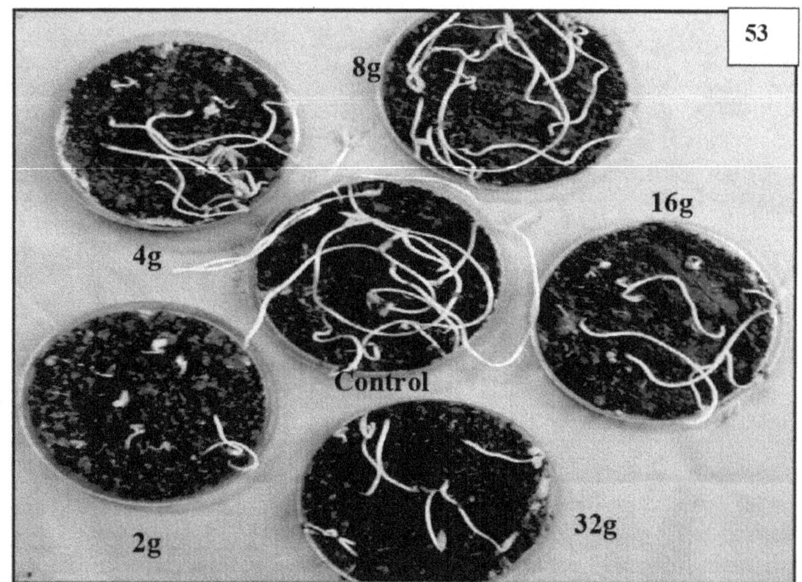

Fig. No.53: Decomposition bioassay: *Phaseolus* seeds showing relative length in different quantities of compost of *Coccinia grandis*.

Plate No. XXII

Table No. 10: Inhibitory effects of Decomposition of *Coccinia grandis* on *Phaseolus aconitifolius* seeds.

Quantity of plant parts in decomposition (g/250g soil)	Radicle Length Mean (cm)			Radicle Length (Mean ± SE)	Hypocotyls Length Mean (cm)			Hypocotyls Length (Mean ± SE)	Average Seed Germination (%)
	I	II	III		I	II	III		
Control	9.62	10.4	10.4	10.1 ± 0.2^a	11.60	12.7	12.5	12.2 ± 0.3^a	96.66
2g	7.12	7.24	7.91	7.4 ± 0.2^b	9.56	9.81	10.6	9.9 ± 0.3^b	96.66
4g	6.52	6.49	7.06	6.6 ± 0.1^c	8.32	9.16	9.26	8.9 ± 0.2^b	96.66
8g	4.16	4.64	4.98	4.5 ± 0.2^d	6.15	7.09	7.37	6.8 ± 0.3^c	90.00
16g	2.43	2.77	2.67	2.6 ± 0.1^e	3.84	4.52	4.78	4.3 ± 0.2^d	76.66
32g	1.10	2.18	1.62	1.6 ± 0.3^f	1.63	3.23	3.09	2.6 ± 0.5^e	63.33

Data were analyzed by one-way ANOVA: Duncan Multiple Range Test (DMRT) using SPSS software. Data of Radicle and Hypocotyls were expressed by Mean±SE ($n = 3$). Values followed by the same letter were not significantly different at 5% level (DMRT).

4) Volatilization: Soil kept with plant material in airtight jar affects seed germination and seedling growth more than in water. It indicates that some volatile substances absorbed by soil particles affect seed germination and seedling growth of test crop. Soil kept with plant material of *Coccinia grandis* in airtight jar affects significantly on seed germination and seedling growth than water. It also indicates that soil absorbs some volatile substance(s)morefrom the plant which are phytotoxins responsible for inhibitory effects. The maximum inhibitory effects on seed germination were observed with *Coccinia* plant material kept with soil. (Table No.14) (Plate No. XXV)

Table No. 14: Inhibitory effects of Volatilization of *Coccinia grandis* on *Phaseolus aconitifolius* seeds.

Types of bioassay	Radicle Length Mean (cm)			Radicle Length (Mean ± SE)	Hypocotyls Length Mean (cm)			Hypocotyls Length (Mean ± SE)	Average Seed Germination (%)
	I	II	III		I	II	III		
Control water	3.76	4.13	3.05	3.6 ± 0.3^a	6.15	6.46	4.88	5.8 ± 0.4^a	96.66
Treated water	2.23	2.29	2.63	2.3 ± 0.1^b	4.22	4.33	4.58	4.3 ± 0.1^b	86.66
Control soil	4.26	4.60	5.00	4.6 ± 0.2^a	6.75	7.32	7.38	7.1 ± 0.2^a	93.33
Treated soil	2.40	2.26	2.35	2.3 ± 0.04^b	4.09	3.87	4.56	4.1 ± 0.2^b	86.66

Data were analyzed by one-way ANOVA: Duncan Multiple Range Test (DMRT) using SPSS software. Data of Radicle and Hypocotyl were expressed by Mean±SE ($n = 3$). Values followed by the same letter were not significantly different at 5% level (DMRT).

PLATE XXV

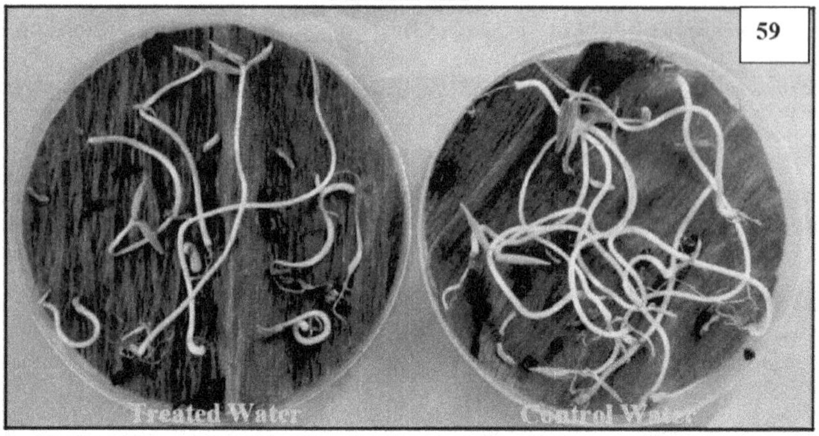

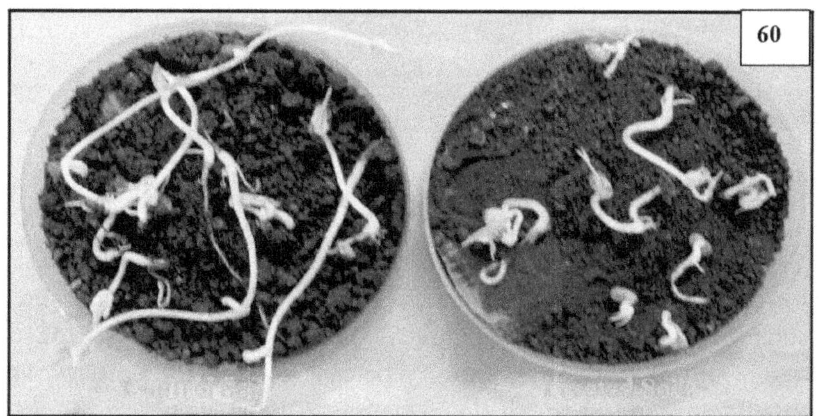

Fig. No. 59: Water Volatilization bioassay of *Coccinia grandis on Phaseolus aconitifolius* seeds.

Fig. No. 60: Soil Volatilization bioassay of *Coccinia grandis* on *Phaseolus aconitifolius* seeds.

5) Root zone soil (Root exudation) Bioassay: The results root zone soil showed considerable inhibition of seed germination and seedling growth of test crop. It was also found that the radicle length was more affected. The root exudates of *Coccinia grandis* show remarkable inhibitory effects on seed germination and seedling growth of test crop. The root exudates significantly affect the radicle and hypocotyls length over control. The major phytotoxicity was observed in radicle length than hypocotyls elongation. (Table No. 18) (Plate No. XXVIII: Figs. 66.)

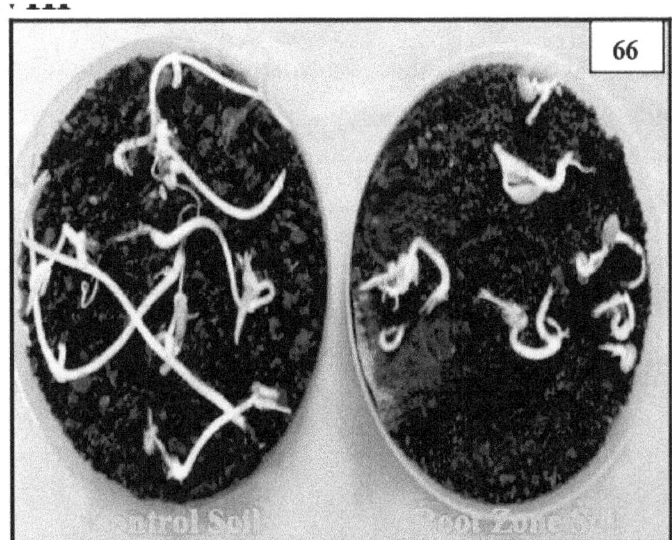

Fig. No. 66: *Coccinia grandis* **Root Zone Soil on** *Phaseolus* **seeds**

Plate No. XXVIII

Table No. 18: Inhibitory effects of Root Exudation of *Coccinia grandis* on *Phaseolus aconitifolius* seeds.								
Concentration (%)	Radicle Length Mean (cm)			Radicle Length (Mean ± SE)	Hypocotyls Length Mean (cm)			Hypocotyls Length (Mean ± SE)	Average Seed Germination (%)
	I	II	III		I	II	III		
Control soil	5.74	4.77	5.21	5.2 ± 0.2	8.45	7.07	7.34	7.6 ± 0.4	100
Root exudation (Root zone soil)	2.92	2.96	2.32	2.7 ± 0.2	5.06	4.62	4.76	4.8 ± 0.1	93.33

6) Root zone soil analysis: The pH value (7.24) was comparatively increased in *Coccinia grandis*. It indicates that some allelochemicals of basic nature may exude from roots of *Coccinia* plants, which inhibites the seed germination of *Phaseolus*. The value of EC (0.15) was much reduced as compare to control soil. There was much remarkable increase in the value of Organic Carbon contents (1.12) over control soil (0.61-0.80). The amount of Phosphorous contents (4 Kg/ac) in the root zone soils also showed appreciable reduction over control soil (51-65 Kg/ac). The amount of Potassium (176 Kg/ac) contents in the root zone soils also showed significant reduction over control soil (240-300). Zinc (1.17 ppm), Copper (0.94 ppm), Iron (4.73 ppm) and Manganese (24.22 ppm) content in the root zone soil of *Coccinia grandis* showed significant reduction as compare to control soil. (Table No. 21)

7) Phytochemical Studies: The root and leaf of *Coccinia grandis* shows presence of proteins, tannins, saponins, flavanoids and alkaloids which acts as allelochemicals. Saponins, tannins, flavanoids and alkaloids were also present in stem of *Coccinia*. The radicle length was more hampered than hypocotyls elongation in all the three phytoextracts and leachates. These phytochemicals might be responsible for allelopathic potential of all three plant parts extract and leachates on seed and seedling growth of test crop. (Table No. 22a)

Table No. 22a. Phytochemical Tests of *Citrullus colocynthis* and *Coccinia grandis*

Test	*Citrullus colocynthis*			*Coccinia grandis*		
	Root	Stem	Leaf	Root	Stem	Leaf
A) WATER EXTRACTS						
Starch	+	-	+	-	-	-
Proteins	-	-	-	+	-	+
Tannins	-	+	+	+	+	+
Saponins	+	+	+	+	+	+
B) ALCOHOL EXTRACTS						
Flavanoids	+	+	+	+	+	+
Alkaloids	+	+	+	+	+	+
Dragendorff's Reagent	+	_	+	-	-	-
Mayer's Reagent	_	_	_	+	_	+

C) *Cucumis trigonus*

1) Phytoextracts Bioassay: Phytoextract study carried out in terms of seed germination and seedling growth of *Phaseolus* seedling showed that, maximum inhibitory effect was found at 1:2.5% of root extract. However, the order of inhibition is root > leaf > stem. The aqueous extract of root and leaf severely suppressed radicle length than hypocotyls of the test crop. The root extracts proved more inhibitory than stem and leaf extract. Aqueous extracts of root and leaf at 2.0% and 2.5% w/v significantly reduces seed germination. All three parts extracts of *Cucumis trigonus* at lower concentration showed drastically increased seedling growth of *Phaseolus*. However, the order of inhibition of phytoextracts of *Cucumis* is root > leaf > stem. (Table No. 3a,b and c) (Plate No. XII, XIII and XIV)

PLATE XII

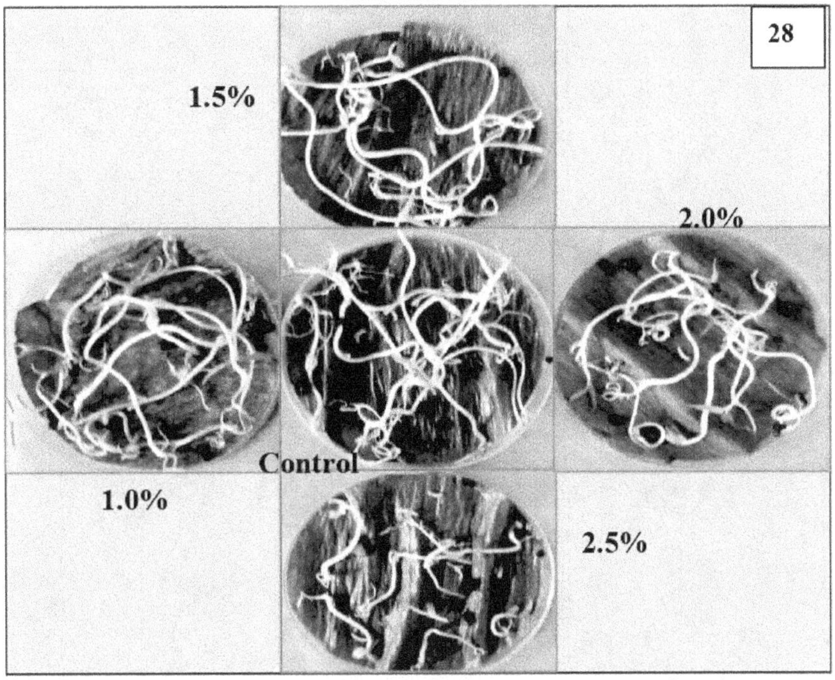

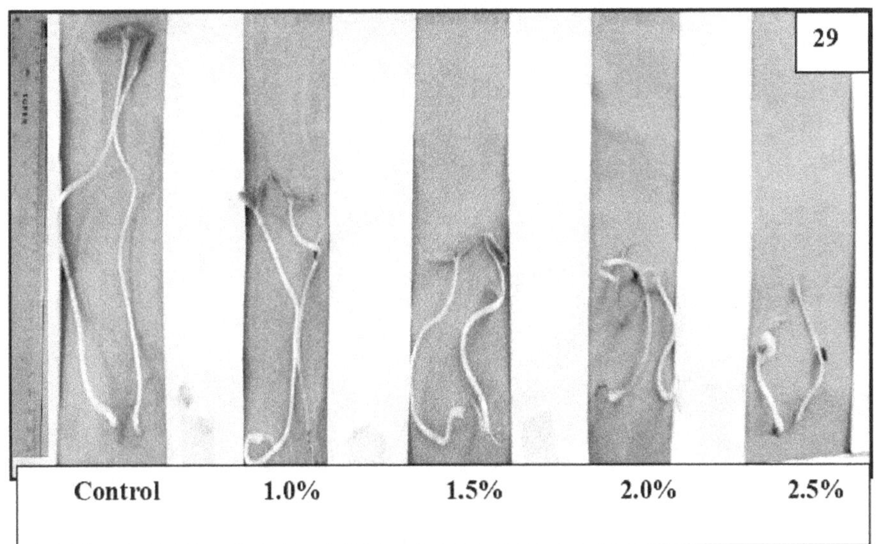

Fig. No.28: Root Phytoextracts bioassay of *Cucumis trigonus*

Fig. No.29: Showing relative length of *Phaseolus aconitifolius* seedling

PLATE XII

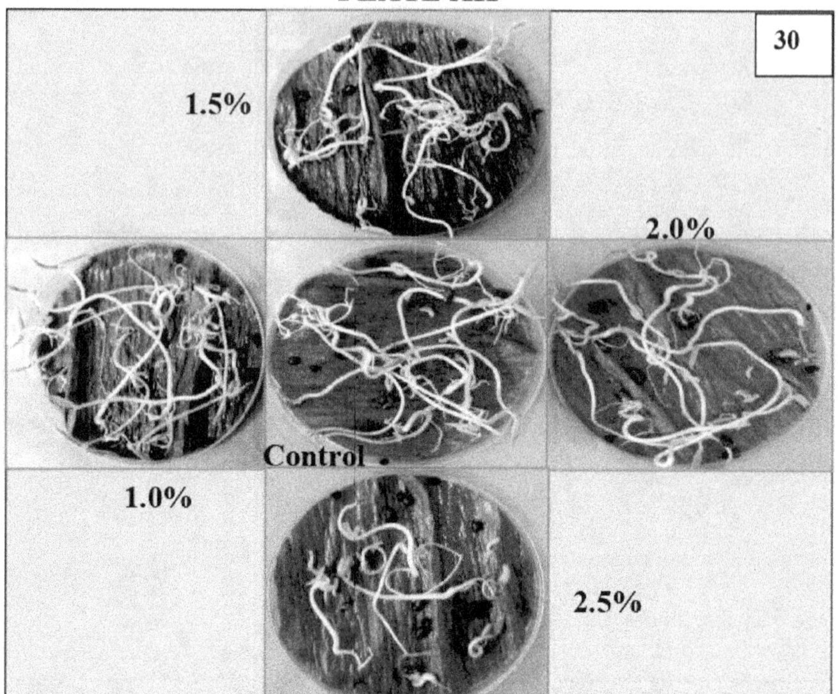

Fig. No.30: Stem Phytoextracts bioassay of *Cucumis trigonus*

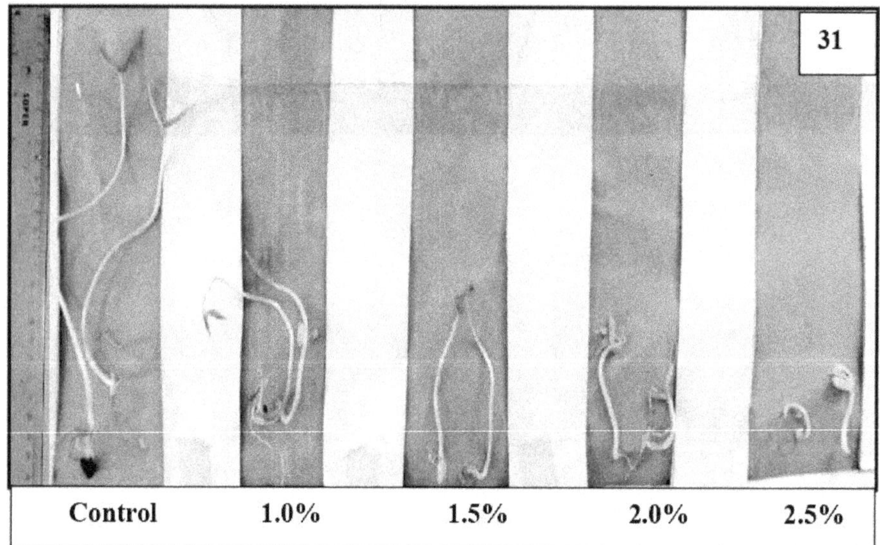

Fig. No.31: Showing relative length of *Phaseolus aconitifolius* seedling

PLATE XIII

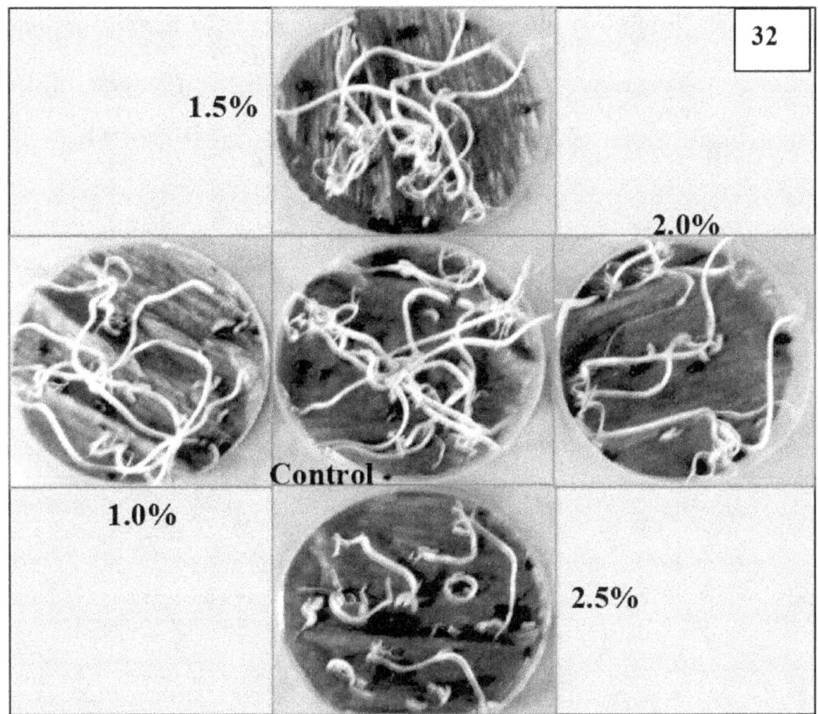

Fig. No.32: **Leaf Phytoextracts bioassay of *Cucumis trigonus***

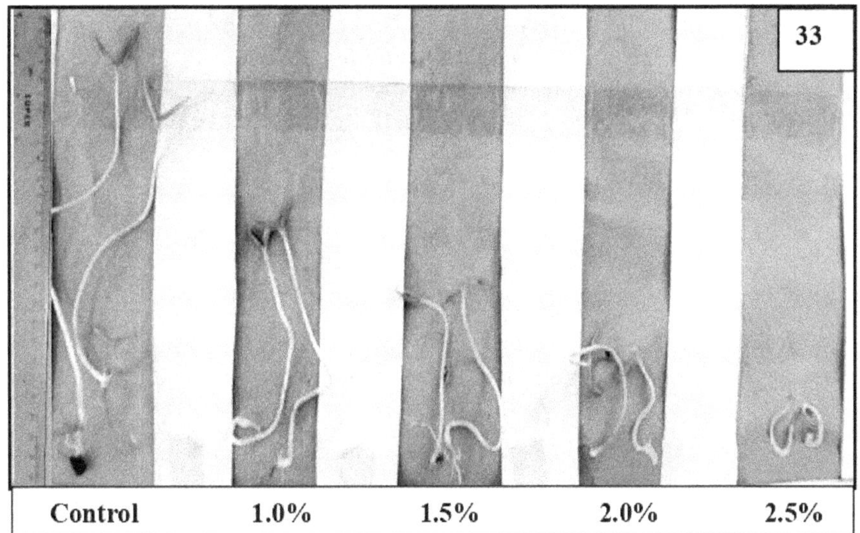

Fig. No.33: **Showing relative length of *Phaseolus aconitifolius* seedling**

Table No.3a: Inhibitory effects of Root Phytoextract of *Cucumis trigonus* on *Phaseolus aconitifolius* seeds.

Extract Concentration (%)	Radicle Length Mean (cm)			Radicle Length (Mean ± SE)	Hypocotyls Length Mean (cm)			Hypocotyls Length (Mean ± SE)	Average Seed Germination (%)
	I	II	III		I	II	III		
Control	6.11	4.58	5.32	5.3 ± 0.4^a	7.68	6.67	7.39	7.2 ± 0.3^a	96.66
1.0%	3.67	3.32	3.58	3.5 ± 0.1^b	6.56	5.18	4.38	5.3 ± 0.6^b	86.66
1.5%	3.05	2.71	2.79	2.8 ± 0.1^{bc}	5.31	4.53	4.61	4.8 ± 0.2^{bc}	86.66
2.0%	2.77	2.02	2.22	2.3 ± 0.2^c	5.06	3.27	3.24	3.8 ± 0.6^{bc}	76.66
2.5%	2.28	1.80	2.17	2.0 ± 0.1^c	4.68	2.80	3.35	3.6 ± 0.5^c	66.66

Data were analyzed by one-way ANOVA; Duncan Multiple Range Test (DMRT) using SPSS software. Data of Radicle and Hypocotyls were expressed by Mean±SE ($n = 3$). Values followed by the same letter were not significantly different at 5% level (DMRT).

Table No.3b: Inhibitory effects of Stem Phytoextract of *Cucumis trigonus* on *Phaseolus aconitifolius* seeds.

Extract Concentration (%)	Radicle Length Mean (cm)			Radicle Length (Mean ± SE)	Hypocotyls Length Mean (cm)			Hypocotyls Length (Mean ± SE)	Average Seed Germination (%)
	I	II	III		I	II	III		
Control	5.25	5.27	5.25	5.2 ± 0.006^a	8.23	8.73	8.23	8.3 ± 0.1^a	100
1.0%	4.50	4.32	4.80	4.5 ± 0.1^b	6.34	6.88	7.31	6.8 ± 0.2^b	96.66
1.5%	4.49	3.36	3.64	3.8 ± 0.3^c	8.30	6.66	7.28	7.4 ± 0.4^{ab}	93.33
2.0%	2.44	2.76	2.72	2.6 ± 0.1^d	4.53	5.05	5.17	4.9 ± 0.1^c	76.66
2.5%	2.71	2.44	2.12	2.4 ± 0.1^d	4.78	4.19	3.57	4.1 ± 0.3^c	70.00

Data were analyzed by one-way ANOVA; Duncan Multiple Range Test (DMRT) using SPSS software. Data of Radicle and Hypocotyls were expressed by Mean±SE ($n = 3$). Values followed by the same letter were not significantly different at 5% level (DMRT).

Table No.3c: Inhibitory effects of Leaf Phytoextract of *Cucumis trigonus* on *Phaseolus aconitifolius* seeds.

Extract Concentration (%)	Radicle Length Mean (cm)			Radicle Length (Mean ± SE)	Hypocotyls Length Mean (cm)			Hypocotyls Length (Mean ± SE)	Average Seed Germination (%)
	I	II	III		I	II	III		
Control	5.50	5.52	6.79	5.9 ± 0.4^a	6.97	7.25	8.45	7.5 ± 0.4^a	100
1.0%	2.98	3.07	3.82	3.9 ± 0.2^b	6.72	5.95	6.52	6.3 ± 0.2^b	90.00
1.5%	3.43	3.32	4.01	3.5 ± 0.2^b	6.72	6.20	5.68	6.2 ± 0.3^{bc}	90.00
2.0%	2.47	2.56	2.14	2.3 ± 0.1^c	5.37	5.03	4.98	5.1 ± 0.1^{cd}	73.33
2.5%	1.35	2.25	1.56	1.7 ± 0.2^c	3.68	5.16	3.63	4.1 ± 0.5^d	83.33

Data were analyzed by one-way ANOVA: Duncan Multiple Range Test (DMRT) using SPSS software. Data of Radicle and Hypocotyls were expressed by Mean±SE (n = 3). Values followed by the same letter were not significantly different at 5% level (DMRT).

2) Leachates Bioassay: The maximum inhibitory effect was caused by root leachates than stem and leaf. It is observed that root leachate suppresses the seed germination upto 50% and overall seedling growth of *Phaseolus*. The root, stem and leaf leachates significantly affect the seed germination and seedling growth of *Phaseolus*. Highest inhibition is found in root leachates followed by stem and leaf leachates. It is observed that the root leachate fully hampered the radicle growth and also suppresses the seed germination. The seedling growth was progressively decreased than seed germination in all three types of leachates. The radicle lengths are more affected than hypocotyls elongation. This may be due to the phytotoxic activity of allelochemicals present in *Cucumis trigonus*. However, the magnitude of inhibition from leachates followed the order: root > stem > leaf. (Table No.7) (Plate No. XX)

PLATE XX

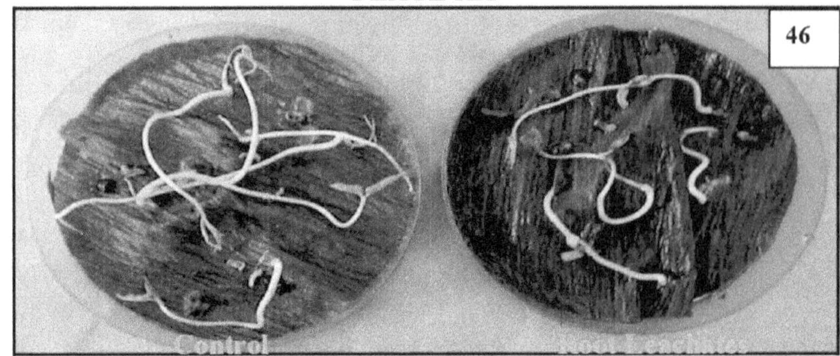

Fig. No.46: *Cucumis trigonus* root Leachates bioassay on *Phaseolus aconitifolius* seeds.

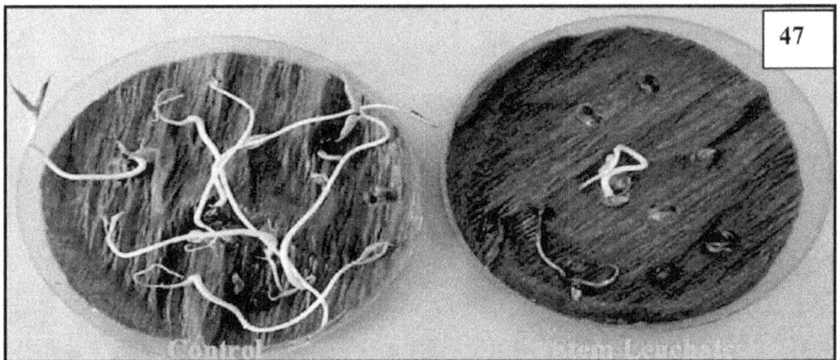

Fig. No.47: *Cucumis trigonus* Stem Leachates bioassay on *Phaseolus aconitifolius* seeds.

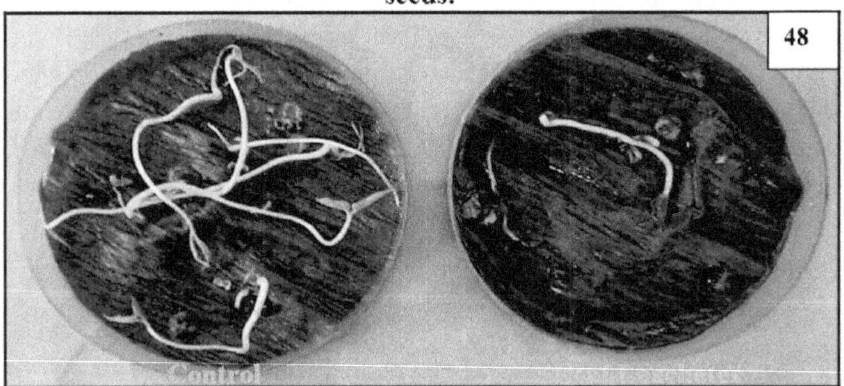

Fig. No.48: *Cucumis trigonus* Leaf Leachates bioassay on *Phaseolus aconitifolius* seeds.

Table No. 7: Inhibitory effects of Leachates of *Cucumis trigonus* on *Phaseolus aconitifolius* seeds.

Types of Leachates	Radicle Length Mean (cm)			Radicle Length (Mean $\pm$ SE)	Hypocotyls Length Mean (cm)			Hypocotyls Length (Mean $\pm$ SE)	Average Seed Germination (%)
	I	II	III		I	II	III		
Control	5.22	4.16	5.56	4.9 ± 0.4^{a}	8.79	7.20	8.11	8.0 ± 0.4^{a}	100
Root	1.18	0.99	0.86	1.0 ± 0.09^{b}	3.09	2.31	2.23	2.5 ± 0.2^{b}	50.00
Stem	1.03	1.05	1.37	1.1 ± 0.1^{b}	2.42	2.75	3.01	2.7 ± 0.1^{b}	63.33
Leaf	1.16	1.18	1.26	1.2 ± 0.03^{b}	2.95	3.07	3.21	3.0 ± 0.07^{b}	70.00

Data were analyzed by one-way ANOVA; Duncan Multiple Range Test (DMRT) using SPSS software. Data of Radicle and Hypocotyls were expressed by Mean±SE (n = 3). Values followed by the same letter were not significantly different at 5% level (DMRT).

3) Decomposition (Decaying plant parts): The decaying plant parts at the rates of 8g, 16g and 32g /250g of soil showed significant reduction in seed germination as well as seedling growth of test crop. Incorporation of dried plant parts in the soil at the lower rates did not show much significant inhibition on seed germination and seedling growth of test crop. The plant material at the higher rates 32g/250g of soil showed maximum reduction in overall seed germination up to 50% and seedling growth. The plant materials at the rate of 8g and 16g showed remarkable inhibitory effect on seed germination and seedling growth. However, the effect of low amount of plant materials at the rates of 2g was not significantly different from the control. In general, the decayed plant parts of *Cucumis trigonus* showed stimulatory effects on hypocotyls length of test crop. Thus, the presence of nutrients in the decaying plant parts may have stimulatory effect on seedling length. (Table No.11) (Plate No. XXIII: Figs 54.)

PLATE XXIII

Fig. No.54: Decomposition bioassay: *Phaseolus* **seeds showing relative length in different quantities of compost of** *Cucumis trigonus.*

Table No. 11: Inhibitory effects of Decomposition of *Cucumis trigonus* on *Phaseolus aconitifolius* seeds.

Quantity of plant parts in decomposition (g/250g soil)	Radicle Length Mean (cm)			Radicle Length (Mean ± SE)	Hypocotyls Length Mean (cm)			Hypocotyls Length (Mean ± SE)	Average Seed Germination (%)
	I	II	III		I	II	III		
Control	8.83	9.06	9.36	9.0 ± 0.1^a	11.4	11.5	11.7	11.6 ± 0.08^a	100
2g	6.83	6.38	5.50	6.2 ± 0.3^b	9.91	9.10	8.09	9.0 ± 0.5^b	90.00
4g	5.00	5.07	4.86	4.9 ± 0.06^c	6.33	6.64	6.49	6.4 ± 0.08^c	80.00
8g	2.92	2.74	3.33	2.9 ± 0.1^d	3.77	3.67	4.41	3.9 ± 0.2^d	73.33
16g	1.76	1.91	2.53	2.0 ± 0.2^e	3.00	3.18	4.42	3.5 ± 0.4^{de}	66.66
32g	0.84	1.08	1.28	1.0 ± 0.1^f	2.20	2.76	3.00	2.6 ± 0.2^e	50.00

Data were analyzed by one-way ANOVA: Duncan Multiple Range Test (DMRT) using SPSS software. Data of Radicle and Hypocotyls were expressed by Mean±SE ($n = 3$). Values followed by the same letter were not significantly different at 5% level (DMRT).

4) Volatilization: During volatilization bioassay soil kept with plant material in airtight jar affects seed germination and seedling growth more in soil as compare to water. It indicates that some volatile substances accumulated in the soil, which causes allelopathic effects on the neighbouring plants. In case of *Cucumis trigonus,* water kept with plant material did not show much more inhibitory effects on seed germination and seedling growth of test crop. Where as soil kept with plant material of *Cucumis trigonus* in airtight jar affects significantly on seed germination and seedling growth of test crop. It indicates that water does not absorb volatile substance(s)from the plant which is phytotoxins responsible for inhibitory effects. (Table No.15) (Plate No. XXVI)

PLATE XXVI

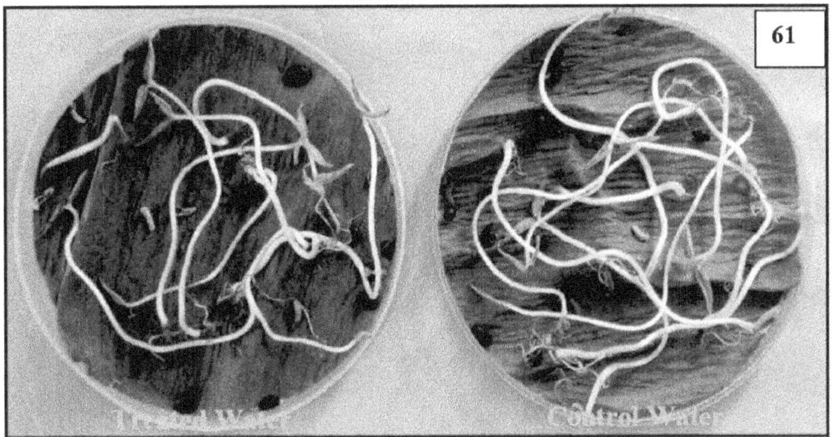

Fig. No. 61: Water Volatilization bioassay of *Cucumis trigonus on Phaseolus aconitifolius* seeds.

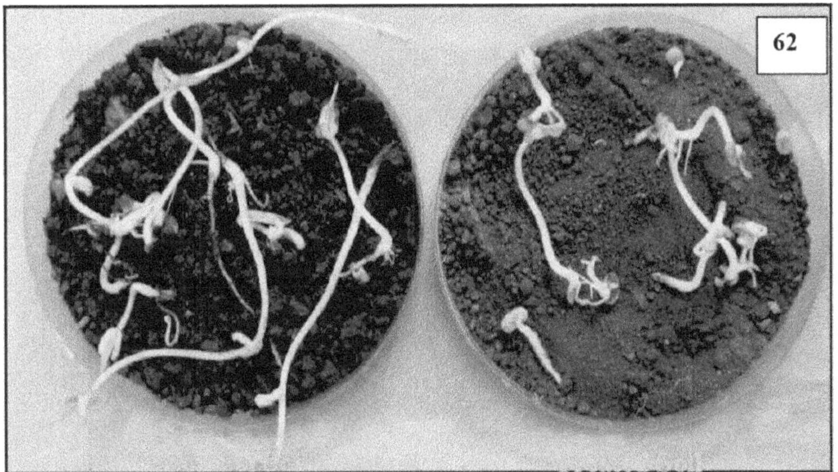

Fig. No. 62: Soil Volatilization bioassay of *Cucumis trigonus* on *Phaseolus aconitifolius* seeds.

Table No. 15: Inhibitory effects of Volatilization of *Cucumis trigonus* on *Phaseolus aconitifolius* seeds.

Types of bioassay	Radicle Length Mean (cm)			Radicle Length (Mean $\pm$ SE)	Hypocotyls Length Mean (cm)			Hypocotyls Length (Mean $\pm$ SE)	Average Seed Germination (%)
	I	II	III		I	II	III		
Control water	4.22	4.50	3.05	3.9 ± 0.4^a	6.74	6.75	4.78	6.1 ± 0.6^a	96.66
Treated water	1.76	2.28	2.63	2.2 ± 0.2^b	3.25	4.25	4.68	4.0 ± 0.3^b	80.00
Control soil	4.67	4.43	5.00	4.7 ± 0.1^a	7.59	7.01	7.18	7.3 ± 0.1^a	93.33
Treated soil	1.95	2.26	2.35	2.1 ± 0.1^b	3.87	3.87	4.66	4.1 ± 0.2^b	83.33

Data were analyzed by one-way ANOVA; Duncan Multiple Range Test (DMRT) using SPSS software. Data of Radicle and Hypocotyls were expressed by Mean±SE ($n = 3$). Values followed by the same letter were not significantly different at 5% level (DMRT).

5) Root zone soil (Root exudation) Bioassay: Bioassay conducted with root zone soil showed decreased radicle and hypocotyls length as well as germination percentage over control. The allelochemicals released from root exudates into the soil showed strong inhibitory effects on seed germination and seedling growth of *Phaseolus*. The radicle length was more affected than hypocotyls growth of *Phaseolus* seedling. However, this plant might release some toxic chemicals through their roots, which inhibites the seed germination as well as seedling growth of test crop. (Table No. 19) (Plate No. XXVIII: Figs 67.)

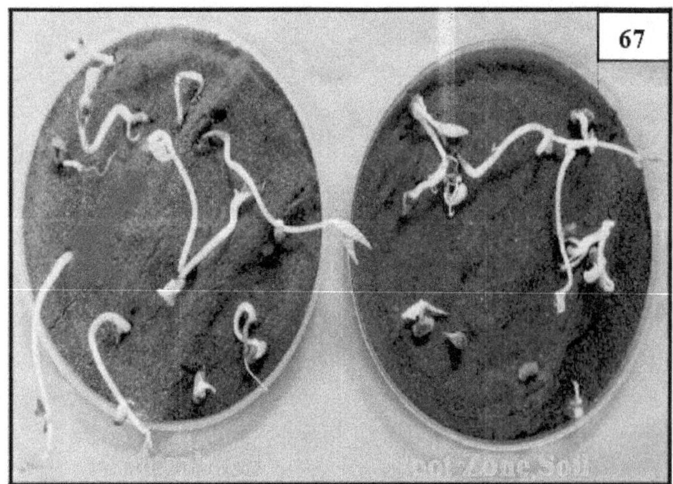

Fig. No. 67: *Cucumis trigonus* Root Zone Soil on *Phaseolus* seeds

Plate No. XXVIII

Table No. 19: Inhibitory effects of Root Exudation of *Cucumis trigonus* on *Phaseolus aconitifolius* seeds.								
Concentration (%)	Radicle Length Mean (cm)			Mean $\pm$ SE	Hypocotyls Length Mean (cm)			Mean $\pm$ SE	Average Seed Germination (%)
	I	II	III		I	II	III		
Control soil	5.94	4.77	5.21	5.3 $\pm$ 0.3	8.92	7.07	7.34	7.7 $\pm$ 0.5	100
Root exudation (Root zone soil)	2.65	3.16	2.20	2.6 $\pm$ 0.2	5.33	4.86	4.52	4.9 $\pm$ 0.2	96.66

6) Root zone soil analysis: The root zone soil pH value (6.78) of *Cucumis trigonus* show acidic in nature. The value of EC (0.28) and Organic Carbon contents (0.36) was much reduced as compare to control soil. The amount of Phosphorous contents (6 Kg/ac) in the root zone soils also showed appreciable reduction over control soil (51-65 Kg/ac). Potassium (189 Kg/ac) contents in the root zone soils also showed significant reduction over control soil (240-300). Zinc (1.28 ppm), Copper (0.38 ppm), Iron (4.65 ppm) and Manganese (26.47 ppm) content in the root zone soil of *Cucumis trigonus* showed significant reduction as compare to control soil. (Table No. 21)

7) Phytochemical Studies: Water extract of root and stem and leaf shows presence of tannins and Saponins. While Alcohol extract of root, stem and leaf shows presence of flavanoids, where as alkaloid was only positive for root and leaf extract. The radicle length was more hampered than hypocotyls elongation in all the three phytoextracts and leachates. All the above chemicals are allelopathic in nature, which indicates that allelopathic chemicals are present in *Cucumis trigonus*. (Table No. 22b)

D) *Diplocyclos palmatus*

1) Phytoextracts Bioassay: Laboratory bioassay studies indicate that aqueous leaf phytoextracts at different concentrations showed significant inhibition on seed germination as well as seedling growth of test crop. The order of inhibition is leaf > root > stem. It is observed that the aqueous extract of leaf at higher concentration strongly inhibited seedling growth as well as seed germination of test crop. But, on the other hand leaf extract at lower concentration had no significant effect on significant effect on germination and seedling growth of *Phaseolus*. However, all the three types of phytoextracts at higher concentration decreased the radicle elongation at appreciable rate than hypocotyls of *Phaseolus*. Root and stem extracts had less inhibitory effct on seed germination than leaf extract. The major toxicity was caused by 2.5% w/v phytoextracts of leaf on both seed germination and seedling growth of test crop. However, the order of inhibition of phytoextracts of *Diplocyclos palmatus* is leaf > root > stem. (Table No. 4a, b and c) (Plate No. XV, XVI and XVII).

PLATE XIV

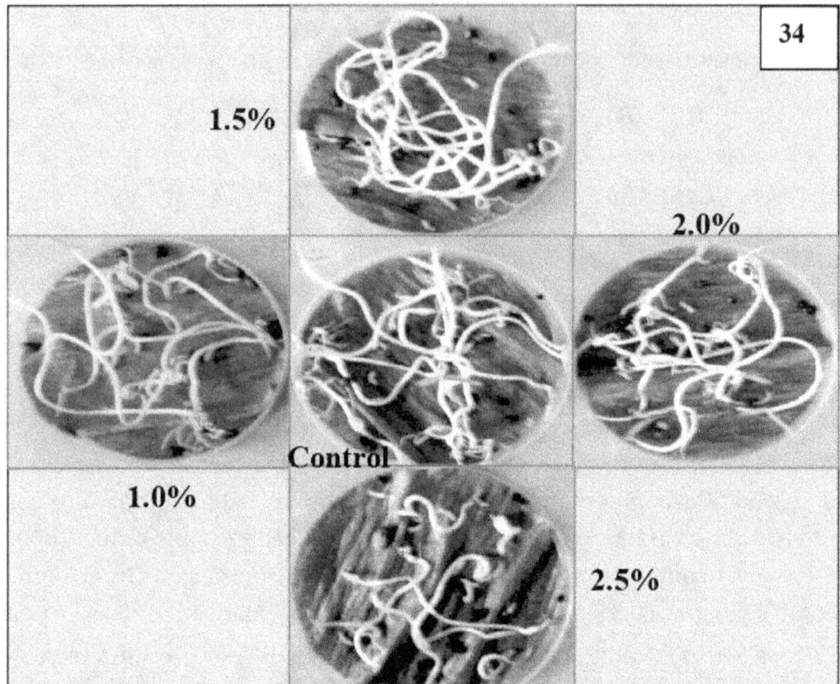

Fig. No.34: **Root Phytoextracts bioassay of *Diplocyclos palmatus***

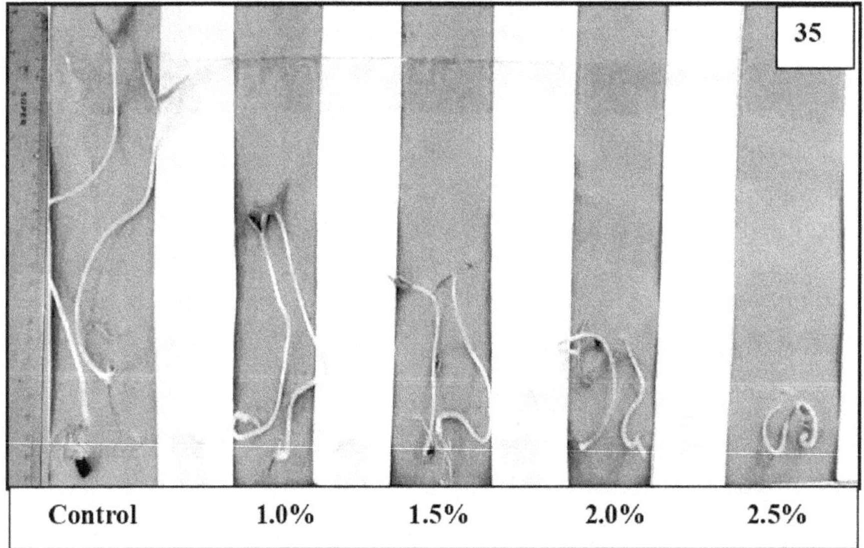

Fig. No.35: **Showing relative length of *Phaseolus aconitifolius* seedling**

PLATE XV

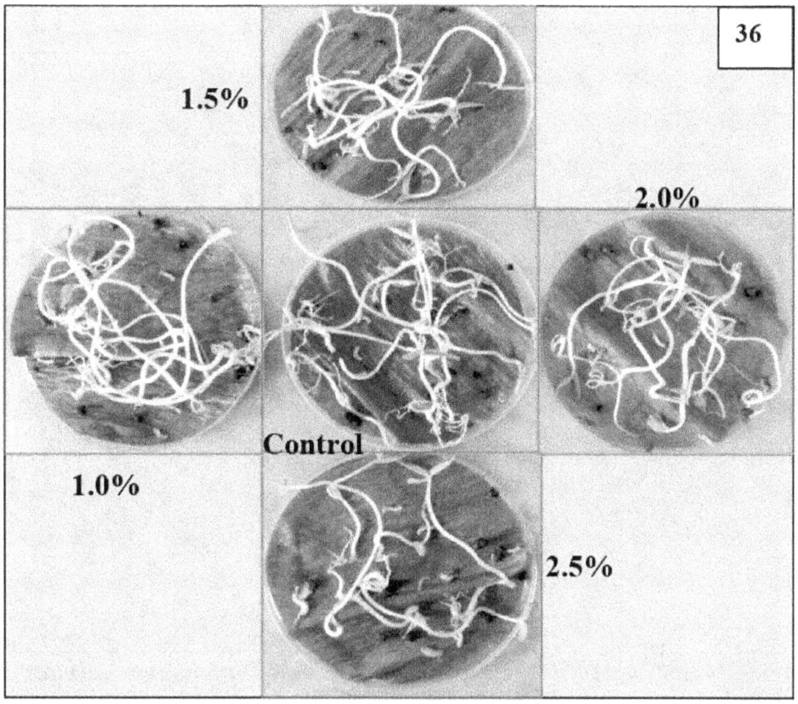

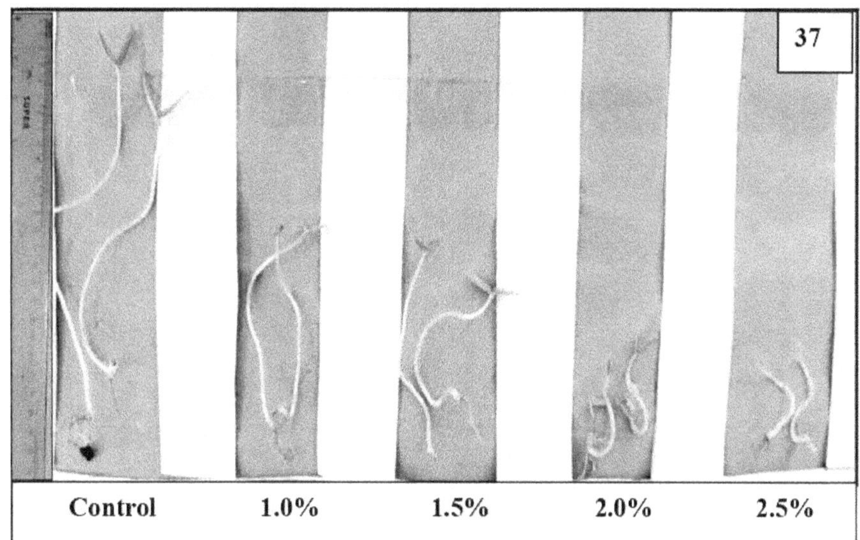

Fig. No.33:Stem Phytoextracts bioassay of *Diplocyclos palmatus*

Fig. No.37: Showing relative length of *Phaseolus aconitifolius* seedling

PLATE XVI

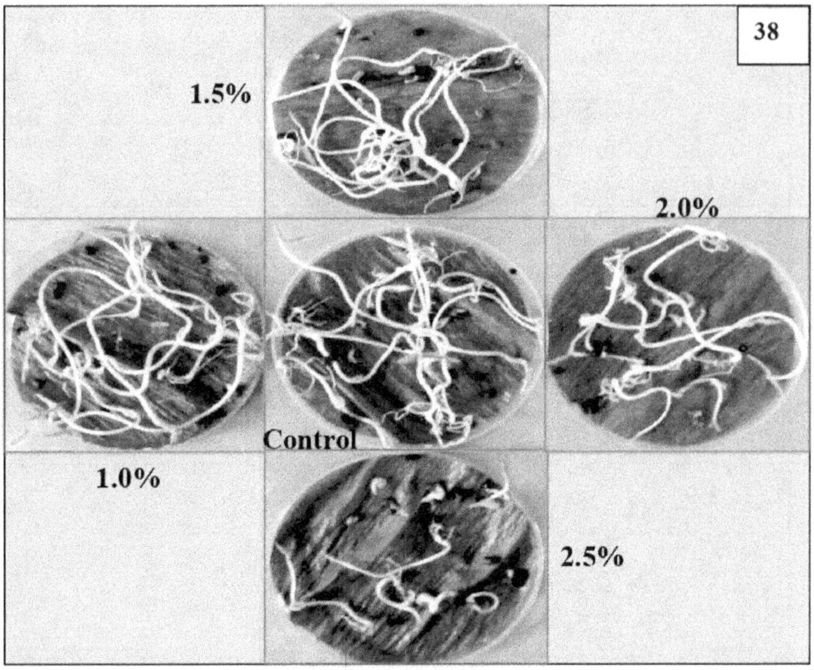

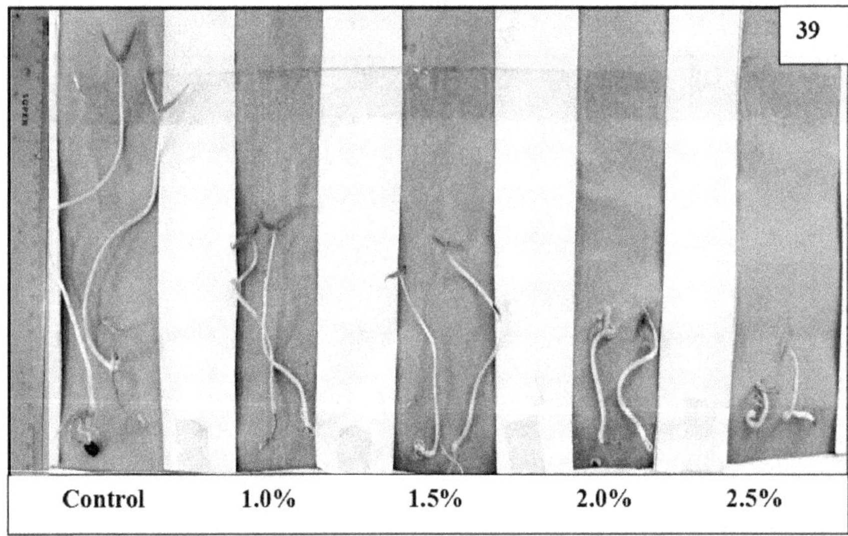

Fig. No.38: Leaf Phytoextracts bioassay of *Diplocyclos palmatus*

Fig. No. 39: Showing relative length of *Phaseolus aconitifolius* seedling

Table No.4a: Inhibitory effects of Root Phytoextract of *Diplocyclos palmatus* on *Phaseolus aconitifolius* seeds.

Extract Concentration (%)	Radicle Length Mean (cm)			Radicle Length (Mean $\pm$ SE)	Hypocotyls Length Mean (cm)			Hypocotyls Length (Mean $\pm$ SE)	Average Seed Germination (%)
	I	II	III		I	II	III		
Control	6.31	6.42	5.88	6.2 ± 0.1^a	7.79	8.22	7.40	7.8 ± 0.2^a	96.66
1.0%	3.70	3.84	3.32	3.6 ± 0.1^c	7.10	7.27	6.40	6.9 ± 0.2^a	86.66
1.5%	5.02	5.18	4.25	4.8 ± 0.2^b	8.21	7.99	6.36	7.5 ± 0.5^a	86.66
2.0%	2.93	3.03	2.36	2.7 ± 0.2^d	5.37	5.63	4.59	5.1 ± 0.3^b	76.66
2.5%	2.73	2.86	2.02	2.5 ± 0.2^d	4.96	5.30	4.79	5.0 ± 0.1^b	76.66

Data were analyzed by one-way ANOVA; Duncan Multiple Range Test (DMRT) using SPSS software. Data of Radicle and Hypocotyls were expressed by Mean±SE ($n = 3$). Values followed by the same letter were not significantly different at 5% level (DMRT).

Table No.4b: Inhibitory effects of Stem Phytoextract of *Diplocyclos palmatus* on *Phaseolus aconitifolius* seeds.

Extract Concentration (%)	Radicle Length Mean (cm)			Radicle Length (Mean $\pm$ SE)	Hypocotyls Length Mean (cm)			Hypocotyls Length (Mean $\pm$ SE)	Average Seed Germination (%)
	I	II	III		I	II	III		
Control	5.28	5.68	5.41	5.4 ± 0.1^a	8.03	8.82	8.65	8.5 ± 0.2^a	100
1.0%	3.89	4.31	4.37	4.1 ± 0.1^b	7.09	7.93	6.87	7.2 ± 0.3^b	93.33
1.5%	3.65	3.99	3.21	3.6 ± 0.2^{bc}	6.00	6.78	6.38	6.3 ± 0.2^{bc}	93.33
2.0%	3.64	3.83	3.01	3.4 ± 0.2^c	5.25	6.25	5.79	5.7 ± 0.2^c	93.33
2.5%	3.38	3.59	2.72	3.2 ± 0.2^c	6.38	5.77	5.13	5.7 ± 0.3^c	86.66

Data were analyzed by one-way ANOVA; Duncan Multiple Range Test (DMRT) using SPSS software. Data of Radicle and Hypocotyls were expressed by Mean±SE ($n = 3$). Values followed by the same letter were not significantly different at 5% level (DMRT).

Table No.4c: Inhibitory effects of Leaf Phytoextract of *Diplocyclos palmatus* on *Phaseolus aconitifolius* seeds.

Extract Concentration (%)	Radicle Length Mean (cm)			Radicle Length (Mean $\pm$ SE)	Hypocotyls Length Mean (cm)			Hypocotyls Length (Mean $\pm$ SE)	Average Seed Germination (%)
	I	II	III		I	II	III		
Control	5.85	6.05	5.89	5.9 ± 0.06^a	8.59	9.05	8.95	8.8 ± 0.1^a	100
1.0%	3.30	3.70	4.11	3.7 ± 0.2^b	7.45	8.63	7.47	7.8 ± 0.3^b	90.00
1.5%	2.88	3.22	2.88	2.9 ± 0.1^c	4.97	5.47	4.97	5.1 ± 0.1^c	83.33
2.0%	2.61	2.83	2.49	2.6 ± 0.09^c	4.84	5.16	4.47	4.8 ± 0.1^c	80.00
2.5%	2.27	2.20	2.00	2.1 ± 0.08^d	5.53	5.35	5.46	5.4 ± 0.05^c	80.00

Data were analyzed by one-way ANOVA; Duncan Multiple Range Test (DMRT) using SPSS software. Data of Radicle and Hypocotyls were expressed by Mean±SE ($n = 3$). Values followed by the same letter were not significantly different at 5% level (DMRT).

2) Leachates Bioassay: The seed germination as well as seedling growth of *Phaseolus* was more hampered by leaf leachates than stem and root leachates. It indicates that leaf leachates containing some water–soluble allelochemicals, which inhibits seed germination and seedling growth of *Phaseolus*. The leachates of root, stem and leaves depressed both seed germination as well as seedling growth of *Phaseolus*. Maximum inhibition is found in leaf leachates followed by stem and root leachates. It is observed that the leaf leachate hampered the radicle growth and also suppresses the seed germination by 66%. While, little effect was observed by stem and root leachates. The radicle lengths are more affected than hypocotyls elongation. The reduction in germination might be due to water – soluble allelochemicals in leaf leachates. (Table No.8) (Plate No. XXI)

PLATE XXI

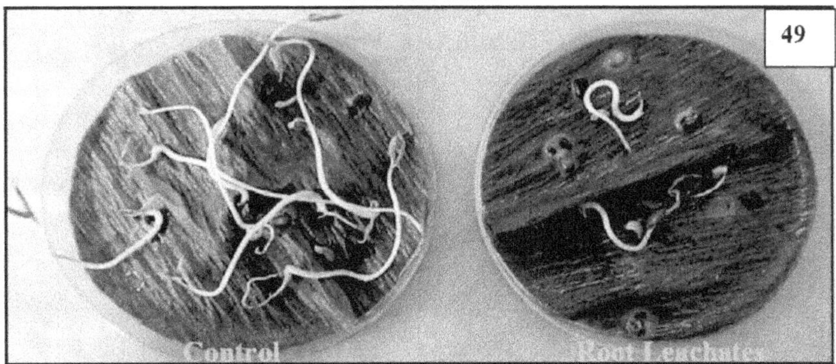

Fig. No.49: *Diplocyclos palmatus* Root Leachates bioassay on *Phaseolus aconitifolius* seeds.

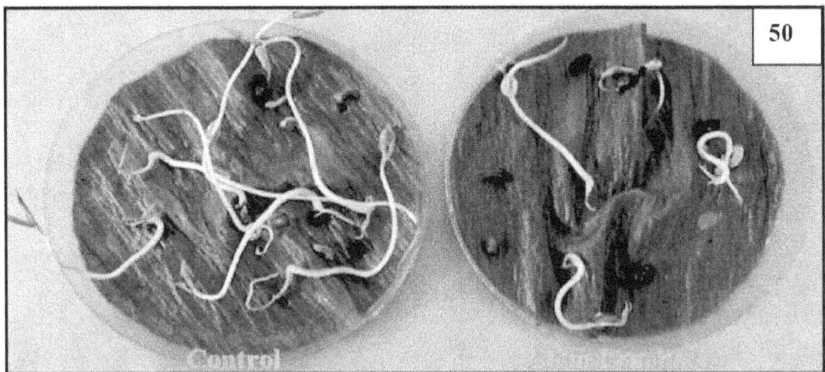

Fig. No.50: *Diplocyclos palmatus* Stem Leachates bioassay on *Phaseolus aconitifolius* seeds.

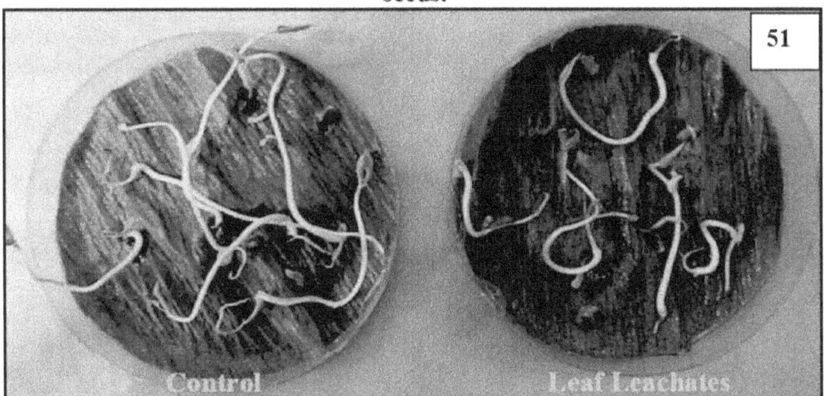

Fig. No.51: *Diplocyclos palmatus* Leaf Leachates bioassay on *Phaseolus aconitifolius* seeds.

Table No. 8: Inhibitory effects of Leachates of *Diplocyclos palmatus* on *Phaseolus aconitifolius* seeds.

Types of Leachates	Radicle Length Mean (cm)			Radicle Length (Mean ± SE)	Hypocotyls Length Mean (cm)			Hypocotyls Length (Mean ± SE)	Average Seed Germination (%)
	I	II	III		I	II	III		
Control	5.66	5.90	5.34	5.6 ± 0.1^a	9.43	9.63	8.81	9.2 ± 0.2^a	96.66
Root	3.06	2.74	2.37	2.7 ± 0.1^b	6.22	5.40	4.68	5.4 ± 0.4^b	80.00
Stem	2.35	2.23	2.15	2.2 ± 0.05^b	6.59	5.10	4.68	5.4 ± 0.5^b	76.66
Leaf	2.58	2.00	1.81	2.1 ± 0.2^b	5.83	4.33	3.83	4.6 ± 0.6^b	66.66

Data were analyzed by one-way ANOVA; Duncan Multiple Range Test (DMRT) using SPSS software. Data of Radicle and Hypocotyls were expressed by Mean±SE (n = 3). Values followed by the same letter were not significantly different at 5% level (DMRT).

3) Decomposition (Decaying plant parts): The decaying plant material at the rate of 16g and 32g/ 250g of the soil showed maximum inhibition on seedling growth of test crop. Where as 32g plant material /250g of soil showed decreased germination percentage. Decaying plant parts mixed with soil significantly reduces seed germination as well as seedling growth. High amount of plant parts (32g) decreased seed germination upto 70%. On the other hand seedling growth was much inhibited in 16g and 32g of plant material incorporated in the soil. The effect of high residue rate was more pronounced on radicle length. However, the decaying plant parts of the weed showed more inhibitory effect on seedling growth than seed germination. It is worth mentioning that test plant seeds grown in the soil incorporated with decayed plant parts showed delayed seed germination over control soil. (Table No.12) (Plate No. XXIII: Figs.55.)

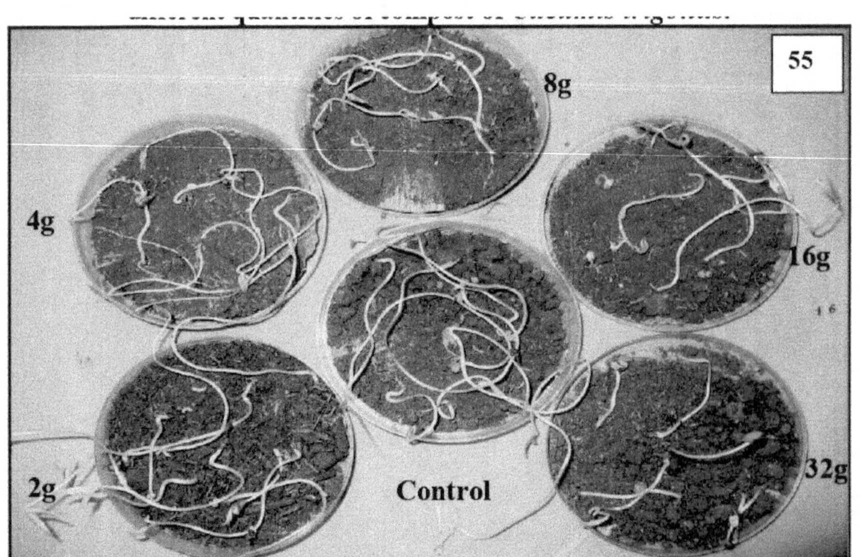

Fig. No.55: Decomposition bioassay: *Phaseolus* seeds showing relative length in different quantities of compost of *Diplocyclos palmatus*.

Plate No. XXIII

Table No. 12: Inhibitory effects of Decomposition of *Diplocyclos palmatus* on *Phaseolus aconitifolius* seeds.

Quantity of plant parts in decomposition (g/250g soil)	Radicle Length Mean (cm)			Radicle Length (Mean $\pm$ SE)	Hypocotyls Length Mean (cm)			Hypocotyls Length (Mean $\pm$ SE)	Average Seed Germination (%)
	I	II	III		I	II	III		
Control	7.94	8.14	9.36	8.4 ± 0.4^a	10.66	10.49	11.76	10.9 ± 0.3^a	96.66
2g	6.66	5.90	4.68	5.7 ± 0.5^b	9.94	8.93	7.07	8.6 ± 0.8^b	86.66
4g	5.54	5.28	4.35	5.0 ± 0.3^b	6.96	7.28	5.65	6.6 ± 0.4^c	83.33
8g	3.42	2.96	2.92	3.1 ± 0.1^c	4.80	4.32	3.77	4.2 ± 0.2^d	80.00
16g	2.26	2.34	2.25	2.2 ± 0.02^{cd}	4.11	4.31	3.85	4.0 ± 0.1^d	76.66
32g	1.87	2.10	1.45	1.8 ± 0.1^d	4.11	4.30	2.49	3.6 ± 0.5^d	70.00

Data were analyzed by one-way ANOVA: Duncan Multiple Range Test (DMRT) using SPSS software. Data of Radicle and Hypocotyls were expressed by Mean±SE (n = 3). Values followed by the same letter were not significantly different at 5% level (DMRT).

4) Volatilization: Water kept with plant material in airtight jar affects seed germination and seedling growth more than in soil. It indicates that some volatile substances absorbed by water particles affect seed germination and seedling growth of test crop. Water kept with plant material of *Diplocyclos palmatus* in airtight jar affects significantly on seed germination and seedling growth than soil. Which indicates that water absorbs some volatile substance(s)morefrom the plant, which may be responsible for potential of this plant. (Table No.16) (Plate No. XXVII)

PLATE XXVII

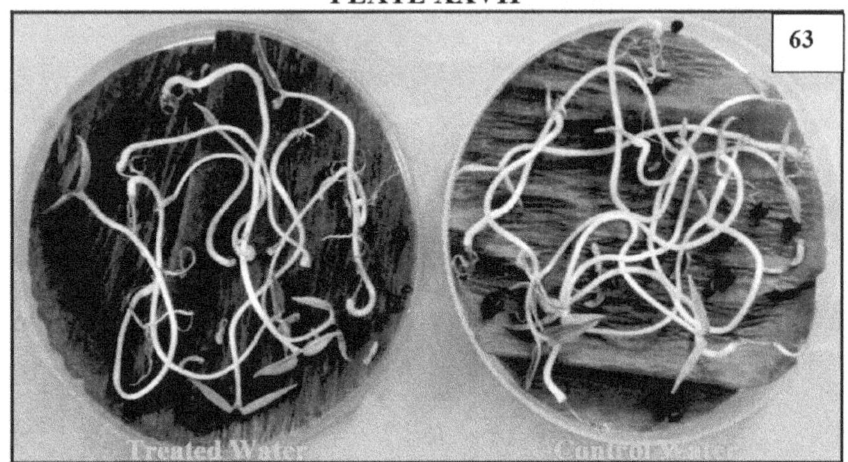

Fig. No. 63: Water Volatilization bioassay of *Diplocyclos palmatus on Phaseolus aconitifolius* seeds.

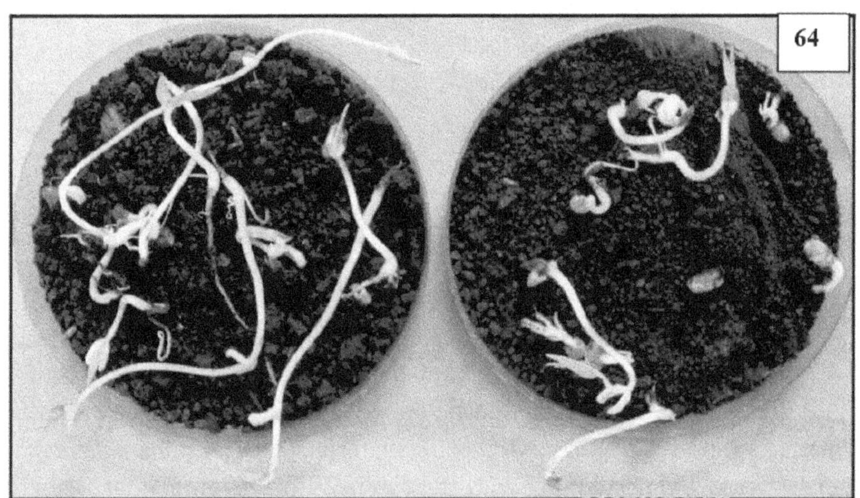

Fig. No. 64: Soil Volatilization bioassay of *Diplocyclos palmatus on Phaseolus aconitifolius* seeds.

Table No. 16: Inhibitory effects of Volatilization of *Diplocyclos palmatus* on *Phaseolus aconitifolius* seeds.

Types of bioassay	Radicle Length Mean (cm)			Radicle Length (Mean ± SE)	Hypocotyls Length Mean (cm)			Hypocotyls Length (Mean ± SE)	Average Seed Germination (%)
	I	II	III		I	II	III		
Control water	4.54	4.09	3.33	3.9 ± 0.3^a	7.26	6.17	5.57	6.3 ± 0.4^a	96.66
Treated water	2.31	2.07	2.91	2.4 ± 0.2^b	3.82	3.77	5.09	4.2 ± 0.4^b	86.66
Control soil	4.94	4.71	5.28	4.9 ± 0.1^a	7.74	7.69	8.07	7.8 ± 0.1^a	100
Treated soil	2.53	2.34	2.63	2.5 ± 0.08^b	4.76	4.05	5.14	4.6 ± 0.3^b	93.33

Data were analyzed by one-way ANOVA; Duncan Multiple Range Test (DMRT) using SPSS software. Data of Radicle and Hypocotyls were expressed by Mean±SE ($n = 3$). Values followed by the same letter were not significantly different at 5% level (DMRT).

5) Root zone soil (Root exudation) Bioassay: During root zone soil bioassay of *Diplocyclos palmatus* seed germination as well as seedling growth of test crop was significantly inhibited over control. The seed germination and seedling growth of *Phaseolus* was severely inhibited by root exudates from soil collected beneath the roots of *Diplocyclos palmatus*. Although the radicle growth was more reduced than hypocotyls elongation by root zone soil collected near the roots of *Diplocyclos palmatus*. (Table No. 20) (Plate No. XXVIII: Figs 68.)

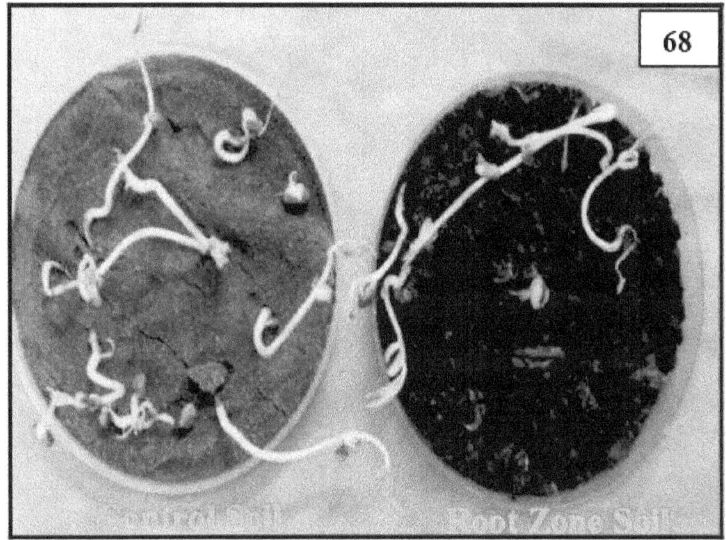

Fig. No. 68: *Diplocyclos palmatus* Root Zone Soil on *Phaseolus* seeds

Plate No. XXVIII

Table No. 20: Inhibitory effects of Root Exudation of *Diplocyclos palmatus* on *Phaseolus aconitifolius* seeds.

Concentration (%)	Radicle Length Mean (cm)			Mean ± SE	Hypocotyls Length Mean (cm)			Mean ± SE	Average Seed Germination (%)
	I	II	III		I	II	III		
Control soil	6.10	5.88	5.45	5.8 ± 0.1	9.04	8.40	7.28	8.2 ± 0.5	100
Root exudation (Root zone soil)	2.95	2.75	2.29	2.6 ± 0.1	5.74	4.27	4.54	4.8 ± 0.4	93.33

6) Root zone soil analysis: The root zone soil pH value (8.34) much increased in *Diplocyclos palmatus* show basic in nature. It indicates that some allelochemicals of basic nature may exude from roots of *Diplocyclos* plants, which inhibites the seed germination of *Phaseolus*. The value of EC (0.19) was much reduced as compare to control soil. There was much remarkable increase in the value of Organic Carbon contents (1.10) over control soil (0.61-0.80). The amount of Phosphorous contents (7 Kg/ac) in the root zone soils also showed appreciable reduction over control soil (51-65 Kg/ac). Potassium (74 Kg/ac) contents in the root zone soils also showed significant reduction over control soil (240-300). Zinc (2.24 ppm), Copper (0.98 ppm), Iron (7.50 ppm) and Manganese (23.10 ppm) content in the root zone soil of *Diplocyclos* showed significant reduction as compare to control soil. (Table No. 21)

Table No. 21. Showing Results of Root Zone Soil Analysis

Sr. No.	Name of the plant species	Soil Parameters								
		PH	EC (at 25C)	Organic Carbon (%)	Total Phosphorus (Kg./ac)	Total Potash (Kg./ ac)	Zinc (ppm)	Total Copper (ppm)	Total Iron (ppm)	Total Manganese (ppm)
1.	Control (Standard Soil)	7.5	1.00	0.61-0.80	51-65	241-300	4-5	5-6	15-20	25-30
2.	*Citrullus colocynthis*	6.13	0.58	0.60	11	154	1.86	3.97	11.18	22.85
3.	*Coccinia grandis*	7.24	0.15	1.12	4	176	1.17	0.94	4.73	24.22
4.	*Cucumis trigonus*	6.78	0.28	0.36	6	189	1.28	0.38	4.65	26.47
5.	*Diplocyclos palmatus*	8.34	0.19	1.10	7	74	2.24	0.98	7.50	23.10

7) Phytochemical Studies: Starch was present only in root, where as tannins, saponins and flavanoids were present in root and stem and leaf of *Diplocyclos palmatus*. Alcohol extract of root and leaf shows presence of alkaloids. These phytochemicals might be responsible for allelopathic effect. The radicle length was more hampered than hypocotyls elongation in all the three phytoextracts and leachates. This might be due to presence of Saponins, tannins, flavanoids and alkaloids. (Table No. 22b)

Table No. 22b. Phytochemical Tests of *Cucumis trigonus* and *Diplocyclos palmatus*

Test	*Cucumis trigonus*			*Diplocyclos palmatus*		
	Root	Stem	Leaf	Root	Stem	Leaf
A) WATER EXTRACTS						
Starch	-	-	-	+	-	-
Proteins	+	+	-	-	+	-
Tannins	+	+	+	+	+	+
Saponins	+	+	+	+	+	+
B) ALCOHOL EXTRACTS						
Flavanoids	+	+	+	+	+	+
Alkaloids	+	-	+	-	+	+
Dragendorff's reagent	-	-	-	-	-	-
Mayer's Reagent	–	–	+	–	+	+

Results of High Performance Thin Layer Chromatography (HPTLC): (Plate XXIX, XXX & XXXI)

With the help of HPTLC technique, three phytoconstituents are identified and confirmed from root, stem and leaves of studied plants. Lupeol was identified and confirmed from stem of *Coccinia grandis* with authentic sample. Terpenoids and Steroids were identified and confirmed in root, stem and leaf of *Citrullus colocynthis, Coccinia grandis, Cucumis trigonus* and *Diplocyclos palmatus* respectively.

PLATE XXIX

Fig. No. 69: Detection of Lupeol from *Coccinia grandis* **with the help of HPTLC**

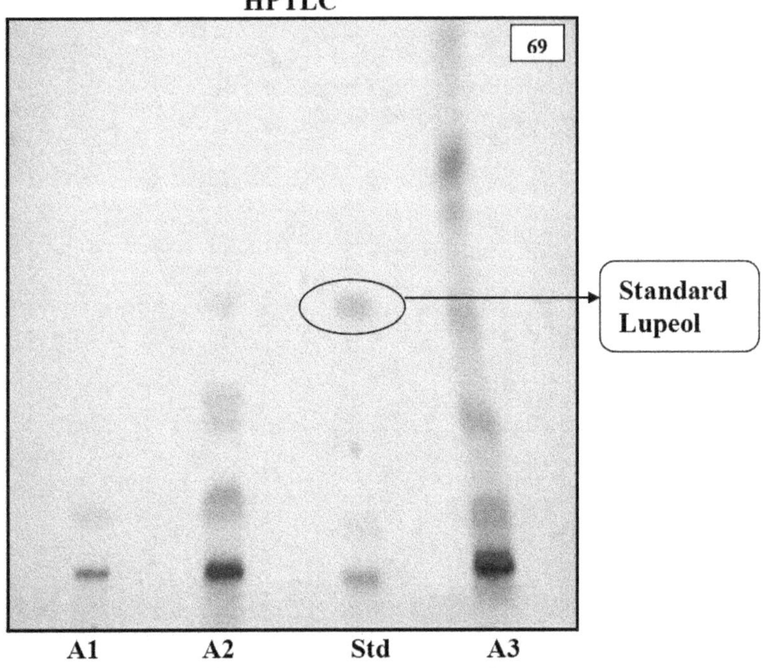

A1 – Root Extract of *Coccinia grandis*

A2 – Stem Extract of *Coccinia grandis*

Std – Lupeol Standard

A3 - Leaf Extract of *Coccinia grandis*

PLATE XXX

Fig. No. 70: Detection of Steroids **with the help of HPTLC**

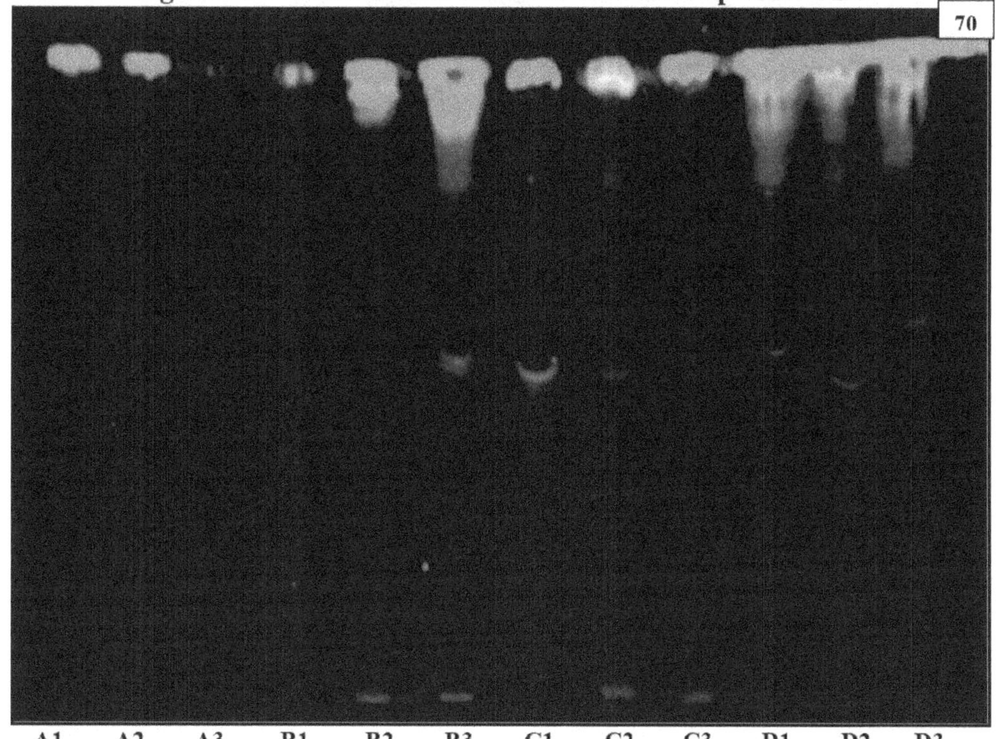

A1 - Root Extract of *Citrullus colocynthis*

A2 - Stem Extract of *Citrullus colocynthis*

A3 - Leaf Extract of *Citrullus colocynthis*

B1 – Root Extract of *Coccinia grandis*

B2 – Stem Extract of *Coccinia grandis*

B3 - Leaf Extract of *Coccinia grandis*

C1 - Root Extract of *Cucumis trigonus*

C2 - Stem Extract of *Cucumis trigonus*

C3 - Leaf Extract of *Cucumis trigonus*

D1 - Root Extract of *Diplocyclos palmatus*

D2 - Stem Extract of *Diplocyclos palmatus*

D3 - Leaf Extract of *Diplocyclos palmatus*

PLATE XXXI

Fig. No. 71: Detection of Terpenoids with the help of HPTLC

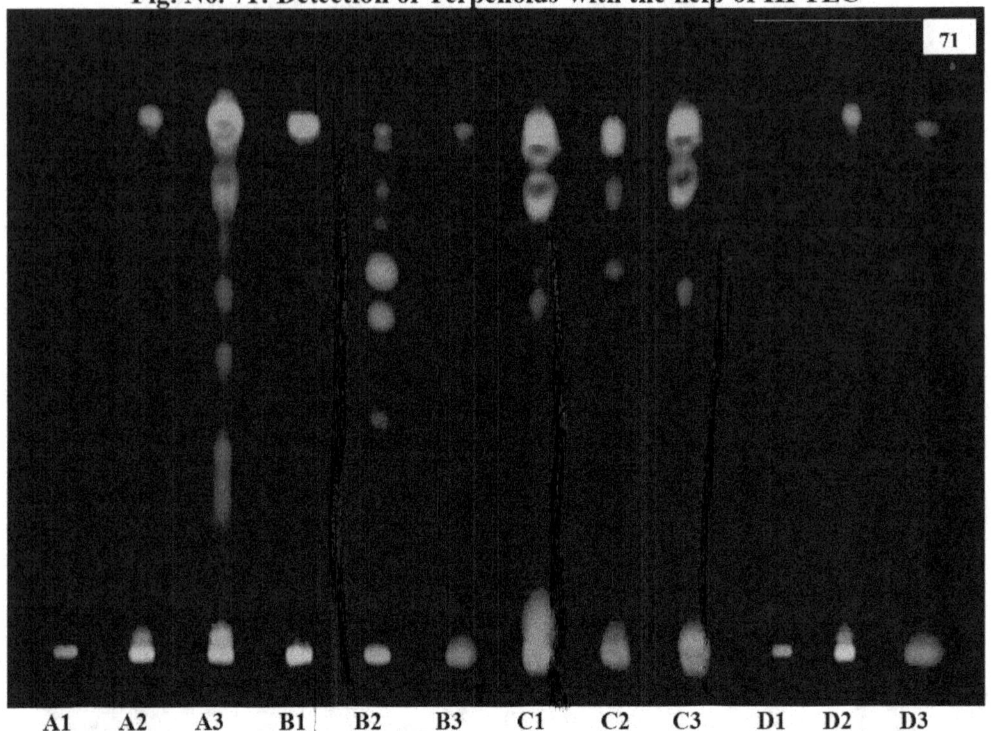

A1 - Root Extract of *Citrullus colocynthis*	**C1 - Root Extract of** *Cucumis trigonus*
A2 - Stem Extract of *Citrullus colocynthis*	**C2 - Stem Extract of** *Cucumis trigonus*
A3 - Leaf Extract of *Citrullus colocynthis*	**C3 - Leaf Extract of** *Cucumis trigonus*
B1 – Root Extract of *Coccinia grandis*	**D1 - Root Extract of** *Diplocyclos palmatus*
B2 – Stem Extract of *Coccinia grandis*	**D2 - Stem Extract of** *Diplocyclos palmatus*
B3 - Leaf Extract of *Coccinia grandis*	**D3 - Leaf Extract of** *Diplocyclos palmatus*

However, all the above said phytochemicals are phytotoxic. The presences of these chemical compounds in the respective plant parts of studied plants were well correlated with the degree of their phytotoxicity. These studies and results indicated that, the allelopathic activity exists in the studied plant part(s) are because of these phytotoxic chemicals.

Comparative Results:

Out of these selected plants the root of *Cucumis trigonus* shows good results in phytoextracts bioassay as compare to other plants. For Leachates and Root Zone Soil bioassays *Citrullus colocynthis* expressed the allelopathic activity on seedling growth and seed germination of *Phaseolus aconitifolius*. But in Volatilization and Decomposition bioassays *Cucumis trigonus* exhibited the allelopathic potency like that of *Citrullus colocynthis*, *Coccinia grandis* and *Diplocyclos palmatus*.

CHAPTER FIVE

Summary & Conclusion

In the present investigation attempts have been made to investigate the allelopathic potency from the selected plants. During the survey it was observed that the selected weeds are noxious weeds in agricultural fields, which significantly reduce the crop yields. It was also observed that though these are the weeds the local people utilities them in various ailments of man and animals. The allelopathic potentials were tested and confirmed by using various techniques such as phytoextracts bioassay, leachates bioassay, root zone soil bioassay, decomposition bioassay and volatilization bioassay on following plants.

1. *Citrullus colocynthis* Schrader. 2. *Coccinia grandis* (Linn.) Voight. 3. *Cucumis trigonus* Roxb. and 4. *Diplocyclos palmatus* (L.) C. Jeffrey.

In addition, soil analysis and detailed phytochemical screening were also carried out and supported to the results which have been obtained in different bioassays. After detailed studies it has been confirmed that these plants are having allelopathic potency as these have been expressed in the fields where they are found to be growing.

Introduction, which deals with the various definition of allelopathy, history of allelopathy, past and present work on allelopathy at national and international level. At the end, applied aspects, scope and future strategies of allelopathy is also mentioned which will be helpful for the farmers to create crop growing awareness, harmful effects from the use of synthetic pesticides. Observations of plants Illustrates morphological descriptions and their medicinal and other uses if any and the results obtained in various experiments. The material and methods used for the this study are of five types of laboratory bioassay, root zone soil analysis and phytochemical studies are also described here. In addition, for the separation and confirmation of allelochemicals HPTLC techniques was also followed. From the observations, results are interpreted and are discussed in this book. However, Laboratory bioassays studies clearly demonstrated that the inhibitory effects of studied medicinal plant parts on seed germination and seedling growth of test crop. Differential degree of inhibitory effects indicated that all plant parts might have different quantities of inhibitory substances with varied chemical nature. Various types of primary as well as secondary metabolites have been studied and are confirmed with the help of phytochemical tests. In the present investigation three chemical constituents are identified and confirmed with the help of HPTLC techniques from the root, stem and leaves of studied plants by using authentic samples. Lupeol, Steroids and Terpenoids are identified and confirmed from root, stem and leaf of *Coccinia grandis,* Steroids and Terpenoids was also identified and confirmed from the root, stem and leaf of *Citrullus colocynthis, Cucumis trigonus and Diplocyclos palmatus.*

Further it is concluded that:

1. The plants selected in the present investigation are allelopathic in nature.
2. The experimental plants show some allelochemicals, such as Lupeol, Steroids and Terpenoids which are identified and confirmed.
3. These plants can be used as pesticides, insecticides, fungicides, etc.
4. It may be helpful for the farmers to create crop growing awareness, harmful effects from the use of synthetic pesticides and also can be used as a repellent in the household to kill mosquitoes, mice, etc.

CHAPTER SIX

References

1. Abdul, A. R. and P. Vankatesan, 2008. Mosquito larvicidal activity of oleic and linoleic acids isolated from *Citrullus colocynthis* (Linn.) Schrad, *Parasitol Res,* **103**: 1383-1390

2. Aldrich, R.J., 1984. Weed – crop ecology: Principle in weed management. *Breton pub., M.A.*

3. Altieri, M.A. and J.D. Doll, 1978. The potential of allelopathy as a tool for weed management in crop fields. *PANS.* **24**: 495-502.

4. An, M.; Pratley, J. E. and T. Haig, 1996. Differential phytotoxicity between *Vulpia* sp. and among individual plant parts. *Allelopathy Journal.* **3**(2): 185-194.

5. An, M.; Zeng, R. S.; Johnson, I. R. and J. V. Lovett, 2003. Modeling aeration effects on plant residue allelopathy. *Allelopathy Journal.* **5**(2): 171-182.

6. Aurora, L.N.; Teresa, R. R.; Jose, L. V.; Vania, B.; Ana, L. A. and R. Cruz-Ortega, 2006. Allelochemical stress causes inhibition of growth and oxidative damage in *Lycopersicon esculentum* Mill. *Plant, Cell and Environment.* **29**(11) 2009-2016.

7. Avchar B.K. 2005. Allelopathic studies in some medicinal plant weeds of agricultural fields in Pune district. Ph.D. Thesis. University of Pune, (M.S.), India.

8. Bell, D. T. and C. H. Muller, 1973. Dominance of California annual grasslands by *Brassica nigra. American Midlands Naturalist.* **90**: 277-299.

9. Bell, D.T. and D. E. Koeppe, 1972. *Agron. J.* **64**: 321 – 325.

10. Bhandari, D. C. and D. N. Sen, 1983. *Indian Rev. Life Sci.* **3**: 207-245.

11. Bhowmik, P. C. and F. D. Doll, 1983a. *J. Chem. Ecol.* **9**: 1263-1280.

12. Bhowmik, P. C. and F. D. Doll, 1983b. *J. Chem. Ecol.* **10**: 161-170.

13. Black, C.A. 1965. Methods in Soil Analysis Part –I & II. *Amer. Soc. Agron. Inc.* Madison. Wisconsin, USA. 3.

14. Bray, R. H. and L. T. Kurtz, 1945. Determining to total organic and available forms of phosphates in soil. *Soil Sci.* **59**: 39-45.

15. Chevallier, A. 1996. The Encyclopedia of Medicinal Plants: A Practical reference guide to more than 500 key medicinal plants and their uses. *DK Publishing,* New York. 336.

16. Chou, C. H. and G. R. Waller, 1983. Allelochemicals and pheromones. Institute of Botany, *Academic Sinica Monograph Series.***5**: Taipei.

17. Cooke, T. 1958. *The Flora of the Presidency of Bombay,* B.S.I. Calcutta 2nd Edition, I: 558 – 582.

18. Cornard, J.P. 1927. *American Soc. Agron .J.* **19**: 1091 (Abstract).

19. Dao, T. H. 1987. Sorption and mineralization of plant phenolic acids in soil. In Allelochemicals: Role in Agriculture and Forestry (ACS Symposium series No. 330) G.R. Waller, Eds. *American Chemical Society,* Washington, D.C. 358-370.

20. Datta, S. C. and Sinha-Roy, 1983. *Acta Agron.* (Hungariaceae) **32**: 124-129.

21. Davis and Company Parke. 1909. *Manual of therapeutics.* Parke, Davis & Co. 262-266.

22. De Candole, M. A. 1832. *Physiologie Vegetale. Bechet Jeune Lib. Fac. Med. Paris.* **3**: 1474-1475.

23. Delprino, L.; Viola, F.; Caramiello, R. and G. Balliano, 1983. Biosysthesis of Sterols and Triterpenoids in Tissue cultures of *Cucurbita maxima. Planta Med.* **49**: 176-80.

24. Deokule, S.S. and B.D. Kamble, 1984. Weeds of irrigated and non-irrigated agricultural fields of Baramati area in Pune District. *J. Econ. Tax. Bot.* **5**(1): 9-16.

25. Deokule, S. S. 1995. Allelopathy in some medicinal plants-inhibition of germination and seedling growth of certain weeds and agricultural crops of Baramati in Pune District. *I. Biol. Ind.* **6** (1&2): 5-10.

26. Deokule, S.S. 1997. The study of flora of Baramati (Pune), M.S. *J. Ec. Tax. Bot.* **21**(1): 179-210.

27. Dipierro, N.; Mondelli, D.; Paciolla, C.; Brunetti, G. and S. Diperro, 2005. Changes in the ascorbate system in the response of pumpkin (*Cucurbita pepo* L.) roots to aluminium stress. *J. Plant Physiol.* **162**: 529-36.

28. Dodge, A. D. 1987. *Pesticides.* **20**: 301-313.

29. Einhellig, F. A. 1985. Effects of allelopathic chemicals on crop productivity. In P. Hedin (Ed.)

30. Bio regulators for Pest Control. *American Chemical Society*,Washington, DC. 109-130.

31. Einhellig, F. A. and G. R. Leather, 1988. *J. Chem. Ecol.* **14**: 1829-1844.

32. Einhellig, F. A. and P. C. Eckrich, 1984. *J. Chem. Ecol.* **10**: 161-170.

33. Einhellig, F.A. 2002. The physiology of allelochemical action: clues and views. *In Allelopathy, from Molecules to Ecosystems*, M. J. Reigosa and N. Pedrol, Eds. *Sci. Pub.*, Enfield, New Hampshire.

34. Evenari, M. 1949. Germination inhibitors. *Bot. Rev.* **15**: 153-194.

35. Fisher, R. F. 1987. Allelopathy: A potential cause of forest regeneration failure. In G. R. Waller (Eds.), *Allelochemicals*: Role in agricultural and forestry. *American Chemical Society,* Washington, DC. 176-184.

36. Frankel, G. S. 1959. The raison d' etre of secondary plant substances. *Science.* **129**: 1466-1470.

37. Grodzinsky, A.M. 1982. In "Evaluation and Environment" (V.J.A. Novok and J. Mlikovskia, Eds.) *Praha Czeckoslovakia.* 133-143.

38. Grummer, G. 1955. Die gegenseitige Beeiaflussung hoherer pflanzen- *Allelopathie Gustav Fisher Verlag*, Jena.

39. Hao, Z. P.; Wang, Q.; Christie, P. and X. L. Li, 2007. Allelopathic potential of watermelon tissues and root exudates *Scientia horticulturae* **112**(3). 315-320.

40. Harborne, J.B. 1987. Chemical signals in the ecosystems. *Annals. of Bot.*, 60:39 – 57.

41. Heisey, R. M.1990. Evidence of allelopathy tree-of-heaven (*Ailanthus altissima*). *J. Chem. Ecol.* **16**: 2039-2055.

42. Hisashi, K.N.; Ho, L. T.; Teruya, T.; Suenaga, K. and V. C. Duong, 2008Allelopathy and the allelophathic activity of a phenylpropanol from cucumber plants *Plant Growth Regulation.*

43. Hooker, J.D. and B. John, 1878. *Journal of a Tour in Morocco and the Great Atlas*, London. 113.

44. Hooker, J. D. 1894. *Flora of India.* B.S.I. Publication, Calcutta.

45. Horsley, S. B. 1977. Allelopathic interference among plants. II. Physiological modes of action. In H.E. Wilcox and A.F. Hamer (Eds.), Proceedings of 4th North American forest Biology Workshop, School of continuing Education, College of Environmental Science and Forestry, Syracuse, N.Y., 93 – 136.

46. Inderjit and K. M. M. Dakshini, 1992. Interference potential of *Pluchea lanceolata* (Asteraceae): Growth and physiological response of asparagus bean, *Vigna unguiculata* var. *Sesquipedalis. Amer. J. Bot.* **79**: 977-981

47. Inderjit and K. M. M. Dakshini, 1994. Allelopathic effect of *Pluchea lanceolata* (Asteraceae): on characteristics of four soils and tomato and mustard growth. *Amer. J. Bot.* **81**: 799-804.

48. Inderjit and K. M. M. Dakshini, 1995. Quercetin and quercitrin from *Pluchea lanceolata* and their effect on growth of asparagus bean. 86-93.

49. Inderjit and K. M. M. Dakshini, 1996. Allelopathic potential of *Pluchea lanceolata*: A comparative study of cultivated fields. *Weed Sci.* In Press. Rice, E. L. 1984. *Allelopathy.* Academic Press, Orlando, FL.

50. Inderjit and R. D. Moval, 1997. Is separating resource competition from allelopathy realistic? *Botanical Review.* **63**(3): 221-230.

51. Jackson, M. L.1973. *Soil Chemical Analysis.* Prentice Hall of India Pvt. Ltd., New Delhi. 134-182.

52. Kaminsky, R. 1981. The microbial origin of the allelopathic potential of *Adenostoma fasciculatum* H & A., *Ecol. Monogr.* **51**: 365-382.

53. Khose, R.G. 2006. Allelopayhic studies in Euphorbiaceae. Ph.D. Thesis. University of Pune. (M.S.), India.

54. Krebs, C. J. 1978. *Ecology: The experimental Analysis of Distribution and Abundance,* Second Edition. Harper and Row, New York.

55. Lawrey, J. D. 1995. Lichen allelopathy: A review, in Inderjit; K.M.M. Dakshini and F.A. Einhellig. (Eds.), Allelopathy: Organism processes and applications. *American Chemical Society,* Washington. DC. 26-38.

56. Li, M.; Ma, Y. and J. Shui, 2005. Allelopathic effects of cultured *Cucurbita moschata* roots exudates. *Ying Yong Sheng Tai Xue Bao.* **16**: 744-9.

57. Lindsay, W. L. and W.A. Norvell, 1978. Development of DTPA soil test for zinc, iron, manganese and copper. *Soil Sci. Soc. Am. J.* **42**: 421-428.

58. Lovett, J. V.1983. In *"Proc. 10th Int. Cong. Prof."* 838.

59. Macias, F. A. 2002. New approaches in allelopathy, challenge for the new millenium. *Third World Congress Allelopathy Abstracts.* **38**.

60. McCalla, T. M. and F. A. Haskins, 1964. *Bactoriol.* Rev. **28**: 181-207.

61. McCalla, T. M. and F. A. Norstadt, 1974. *Agri. Environ.* **1**: 153-174.

62. Mehrnaz, A. B. 2008. The importance of using the extract of *Hanzal* as inhibitors in paper manuscripts. *Fourth Islamic Manuscript Conference,* Queen's College, University of Cambridge.

63. Molisch, H.1937. *"The influence of one plant on another: Allelopathy".* Edited by Narwal, S.S. (2001), Translated by L. J. La Fleur & M.A. Bari Malik. Scientific Publisher, Jodhpur, (India).

64. Mufti, A. U.; Key-Sun, K. and G. Y. Yeon, 2006. Purification and characterization of a serine protease from Cucumis trigonus Roxburghi. Phytochemistry 67(9): 870-875

65. Mullai, K. and A. Jebanesan, 2007. Larvicidal, ovicidal and repellent activities of the leaf extract of two cucurbitaceae plants against filarial vector *Culex quinquefasciatus* (Say) (Dipteria: Culicidae). *Trop Biomed.* **24**(1):1-6.

66. Muller, C. H. 1969. Allelopathy as a factor in ecological process. *Vegetatio.* **18**: 348-357.

67. Muller, C.H. 1966. The role of Chemical inhibition (allelopathy) in vegetational composition. *Bull Torrey Bot.* **93**: 332-335.

68. Nadkarni, A. K. 2002. *K.M.Nadkarni's Indian Materia Medica,* Popular Prak. Pvt. Ltd. Bombay. **I**: 220-405.

69. Narwal, S.S. and P. Touro, 1994. *Allelopathy in Agriculture and Forestry.* Jodhpur, India: Scientific Publishers. 312.

70. National Research Council, 2006. "Egusi", *Lost Crops of Africa. Vegetables.* National Academies Press.Lost Crops of Africa. **2**.

71. Overland, L. 1966. The role of allelopathic substances in the 'smother crop' barley. *Amer. J. Bot.* **53**: 423.

72. Passera, C.A.; Pedrotti and G. Ferrari, 1964. *Chromatography.* **14**: 289.

73. Patrick, Z. A. and L. W. Koch, 1958. *Canadian T. Bot.* **36**: 621-647.

74. Patrick, Z. A.; Toussous, T. A. and L. W. oval Koth, 1964. *Ann. Rev. Phytopathol.* **2**: 267-292.

75. Peach and K. V. Tracy. 1955. *Modern Methods of Plant Analysis. Springer* Ver., **2**: 153-154.

76. Peng, S.; Chen, Z.; Wen, J. and H. Shao, 2004. Is allelopathy a driving force in forest succession? *Allelopathy Journal.* **14**(2): 197-204.

77. Peterson, J. K. and H. F. Harrison, 1994. Bioassay guided evaluation of constitutive inhibitors in yellow squash (*Cucurbita pepo* L.) *Allelopathy Journal.* **1**(1): 41-46.

78. Putnam, A. R. and C. S. Tang, 1986. *Allelopathy: State of the Science: in the Science of Allelopathy* (John, Wiley and Sons. INC). 1-17.

79. Putnam, A. R. and L. A. Weston, 1986. Adverse impacts of allelopathy in agricultural systems. *In The Science of Allelopathy*, Eds. A. R. Putnam and C. S. Tang. John W. & Sons, New York. 43-56.

80. Putnam, A. R. and W. B. Duke, 1978. *Ann. Rev. Phytopathol.* **16**: 431-451.

81. Putnam, A.R. 1985. Allelopathic research in agriculture: past highlights and potential. In 'The Chemistry of Allelopathy' Eds. A.C. Thompson, ACS Symposium Series No. 268, *American Chemical Soc.* Washington, D.C. 1-8.

82. Putnam, A.R. and W. B. Duke, 1974. Biological Suppression of weeds: Evidence for allelopathy in accessions of cucumber. *Science.* **185**: 370-372.

83. Rice, E. L. 1964. Inhibition of nitrogen fixing and nitrifying bacteria by seed plants. *J. Ecology.* **45**: 824-837.

84. Rice, E. L. 1974. *Allelopathy,* Academic Press, New York.

85. Rice, E. L. 1979. *Allelopathy-* an update. *Bot. Rev.* **45**: 15-109.

86. Rice, E. L. 1984. *Allelopathy*, Academic Press, Orlando, FL. 422.

87. Rice, E. L. 1985. *Allelopathy,* Academic Press, Orlando, Florida. **1**:131.

88. Rice, E. L.1986. Allelopathy growth stimulation. In: The Science of Allelopathy, (Eds.), A.R. Putnam and C.S. Tang, John Wiley., New York, 23 – 42.

89. Ricklefs, R. E. 1979. *Ecology.* Second Eds. Chiron press.

90. Riddle and M. John. 1999. Eve's Herbs: A History of Contraception and Abortion in the West. Harvard University Press.

91. Romero-Romera, T.; Sanchez-Nieto, S.; Sanjuan-Badillo, S.; Anaya, A. L. and R. Cruz-Ortega,2005. Comparative effects of allelochemicals and water stress in roots of *Lycopersicon esculentum* Mill. (Solanaceae). *Plant.* **168**(4): 1059-1066.

92. Roshchina, V. V. and E. V. Melnikova, 1998. Allelopathy and plant reproductive cells: participation of acetocholine and histamine in signaling in the interactions of pollen and pistil. *Allelopathy Journal.* **5**(2): 171-182.

93. Rovira, A. D.1969. Plant root exudates. *Ibid.* **35**:35-59.

94. Santapau, H. 1957. *The Flora of Purandhar.* B.S.I. Publication, Calcutta.

95. Schreiner, O. and E. C. Lathrob, 1911. Examination of soils for organic constituents. *USDA Bur. Soils Bull.* 80.

96. Schreiner, O. and E. D. Shorey, 1909. The isolation and harmful substances from soil. *USDA Bur. Soils. Bull.* 53.

97. Schreiner, O. and H.S. Reed, 1907. Certain organic constituents of soil in relation to Soil fertility. *USDA Bur. Soils. Bull.* 47.

98. Schreiner, O. and M. X. Sullivan, 1909. *J. Boil. Chem.* **6**: 39-50.

99. Sen, D. N. 1982. Environment and plant life in Indian desert. *GEOBIOS*, Jodhpur, India. 249.

100. Sethi, P. D.1996. *High Performance Thin Layer Chromatography.* CBS Publicshers and Distributors, New Delhi. 3-68.

101. Shukla, R.; Chakravarty, M. and M. P. Gautam, 2008. Indigenous medicine used for treatment of gynecological disorders by tribal of Chhattisgarh, India. *J. of Med.Plants Res.* **2**(2): 356-360.

102. Singh, H. P.; Batish, D. R. and R. K. Kohli, (2001). *Allelopathy in agroecosystems*: an overview. In Allelopathy in Agroecosystems, Eds. R. K. Kohli; H. P. Singh and D. R. Batish. The Haworth Press, New York. 1-41.

103. Smith, A. M. and D. M. Secoy, 1977. *Furrow.* **13**: 27.

104. Stahl, E. 1969. *Thin Layer Chromatography A Laboratory Handbook. Springer,* Verlog Berlin, Heidenberg.

105. Tivy, J. 1971. *Biogeography.* A study of plant in the Ecosphere. Oliver and Boyd, Edinburgh. 394.

106. Trease, G. E. and W. C. Evans, 1972. *Pharmacognosy.* 10th Eds. Bailer Tindall, London.

107. Turkey, H. B. (Jr.) 1962. Loss of organic and inorganic materials by leaching from leaves and other ground plant parts. *International Atomic Energy Agency.* Vienna. 289 – 302.

108. Turkey, H. R. (Jr.) 1964. The occurrence of leaching from above ground plant parts and nature of the material. *Leached Proc. XVI International Horticultural Congress.* **4**: 164-153.

109. Verma, S. C.1938. On the nature of the competition between plants in the early phases of their development. *Ann. Bot.* **2**: 203-225.

110. Waller, G. R. 1987. Allelochemicals: Role in agricultural and forestry. ACS Symposium Series. *American Chemical Soc.* Washington, DC. **330.**

111. Wang, T. S. C.; Cheng, S.Y. and H. Tung, 1967. *Soil Science.* **104**: 138-144.

112. Whittakar, R. H. 1971. The chemistry of communities. In: Biochemical interactions among plants. Eds. *U S Nat. Com. Fer. IBP. Nat. Acad. of Sci.,* Washington, DC. 10-18.

113. Whittaker, R. H. 1975. (Second Edition) *Communities and Ecosystems:* McMillan Publishing Company. Inc. New York; Collier McMillan Publishers, London.

114. Whittaker, R. H. and P. P. Fenny, 1971. *Allelochemicals*: Chemical interactions between species. *Science.* **171**: 757-770.

115. Willis, R. J. 1994. Terminology and trends in allelopathy. *Allelopathy Journal.* **1**(1): 6-28.

116. Willis, R. J. 1997. The history of allelopathy. 2. The second phase (1900-1920). The era of S. U. Pickering and the USDA Bureau of Soils. *Allelopathy Journal.* **4**: 7-56.

117. Willis, R. J. 2000. *Juglans* spp., juglone and allelopathy. *Allelopathy Journal.* **7**: 1-55.
118. Woods, F.W. 1960. Biological antagonism due to phytotoxic root exudates. *Bot. Rev.* **26**: 546-569.